D0762546

Computer Science Programming Basics with Ruby

Ophir Frieder, Gideon Frieder, and David Grossman

The Property of
The MASTERS Program
Charter School

O'REILLY®

Beijing · Cambridge · Farnham · Köln · Sebastopol · Tokyo

Computer Science Programming Basics with Ruby

by Ophir Frieder, Gideon Frieder, and David Grossman

Copyright © 2013 Ophir Frieder, Gideon Frieder, and David Grossman. All rights reserved.

Printed in the United States of America.

Published by O'Reilly Media, Inc., 1005 Gravenstein Highway North, Sebastopol, CA 95472.

O'Reilly books may be purchased for educational, business, or sales promotional use. Online editions are also available for most titles (*http://my.safaribooksonline.com*). For more information, contact our corporate/institutional sales department: 800-998-9938 or *corporate@oreilly.com*.

Editors: Simon St. Laurent and Meghan Blanchette	**Cover Designer:** Randy Comer
Production Editor: Holly Bauer	**Interior Designer:** David Futato
Copyeditor: Audrey Doyle	**Illustrators:** Rebecca Demarest and Kara Ebrahim
Proofreader: Julie Van Keuren	

April 2013:   First Edition

Revision History for the First Edition:

2013-04-15:   First release

See *http://oreilly.com/catalog/errata.csp?isbn=9781449355975* for release details.

Nutshell Handbook, the Nutshell Handbook logo, and the O'Reilly logo are registered trademarks of O'Reilly Media, Inc. *Computer Science Programming Basics in Ruby*, the image of a common Creeper, and related trade dress are trademarks of O'Reilly Media, Inc.

Many of the designations used by manufacturers and sellers to distinguish their products are claimed as trademarks. Where those designations appear in this book, and O'Reilly Media, Inc., was aware of a trademark claim, the designations have been printed in caps or initial caps.

While every precaution has been taken in the preparation of this book, the publisher and authors assume no responsibility for errors or omissions, or for damages resulting from the use of the information contained herein.

ISBN: 978-1-449-35597-5

[LSI]

Table of Contents

Preface

Computer science introductory texts are often unnecessarily long. Many exceed 500 pages, laboriously describing every nuance of whatever programming language they are using to introduce the concepts.

There is a better way: a programming language that has a low entry barrier. Preferably, the language selected should be a real, widely used language with a subset that is powerful and useful, yet mercifully small. Such a choice should arm the readers with marketable tools. The esoteric details of the programming language, however, should be ignored but with pointers for future investigation provided.

Ruby is a programming language well suited to this task. It is object-oriented, interpreted, and relatively straightforward. More so, instead of being purely educationally oriented, its popularity in industry is steadfastly growing.

Our book should be covered in sequential fashion. Each chapter assumes that the material from the preceding chapters has been mastered. To focus the discussion, we ignore gory details, such as user interface design and development issues, that we believe are ancillary to the core of computer science. Such issues should be, and are, covered in depth in a variety of subsequent courses.

Our target audience is students and practitioners who wish to learn computer science using Ruby rather than just how to program in a given language. This book consistently emphasizes why computer science is different from computer programming. Students and practitioners must understand what an algorithm is and what differentiates differing algorithms for the same task. Although we are living in an era of growing computational resources, we are also living in a world of growing data sets. Data amass every day; thus, efficient algorithms are needed to process these data.

Students and practitioners completing a course using this book possess foundational knowledge in the basics of computer science and are prepared to master abstract and advanced concepts. Second semester courses should rely on languages other than Ruby, furthering the understanding that programming languages are just interchangeable, expressive tools. We know, however, that many students and practitioners may not take another computer science course. If that is the case, this book provides them with an overview of the field and an understanding of at least one popular programming language that happens to be useful from both a practical and a pedagogical standpoint.

Concepts taught in this book provide students and practitioners with a sufficient foundation to later learn more complex algorithms, advanced data structures, and new programming languages.

Finally, we hope to instill a core appreciation for algorithms and problem solving so students and practitioners will solve problems with elegance and inspiration rather than simply plowing ahead with brute force.

The slides corresponding to this book and the source code listed in the book are available at *http://ir.cs.georgetown.edu/Computer_Science_Programming_Basics_with_Ruby*.

Conventions Used in This Book

The following typographical conventions are used in this book:

Italic
>   Indicates new terms, URLs, email addresses, filenames, and file extensions

`Constant width`
>   Used for program listings, as well as within paragraphs to refer to program elements such as variable or function names, databases, data types, environment variables, statements, and keywords

`Constant width bold`
>   Shows commands or other text that should be typed literally by the user

`Constant width italic`
>   Shows text that should be replaced with user-supplied values or by values determined by context

     This icon signifies a tip, suggestion, or general note

Using Code Examples

This book is here to help you get your job done. In general, you may use the code in your programs and documentation. You do not need to contact us for permission unless you're reproducing a significant portion of the code. For example, writing a program that uses several chunks of code from this book does not require permission. Selling or distributing a CD-ROM of examples from O'Reilly books does require permission. Answering a question by citing this book and quoting example code does not require permission. Incorporating a significant amount of example code from this book into your product's documentation does require permission.

We appreciate, but do not require, attribution. An attribution usually includes the title, author, publisher, and ISBN. For example: "*Computer Science Programming Basics in Ruby* by Ophir Frieder, Gideon Frieder, and David Grossman (O'Reilly). Copyright 2013 Ophir Frieder, Gideon Frieder, and David Grossman, 978-1-449-35597-5."

If you feel your use of code examples falls outside fair use or the permission given here, feel free to contact us at *permissions@oreilly.com*.

Safari® Books Online

 Safari Books Online (*www.safaribooksonline.com*) is an on-demand digital library that delivers expert content in both book and video form from the world's leading authors in technology and business.

Technology professionals, software developers, web designers, and business and creative professionals use Safari Books Online as their primary resource for research, problem solving, learning, and certification training.

Safari Books Online offers a range of product mixes and pricing programs for organizations, government agencies, and individuals. Subscribers have access to thousands of books, training videos, and prepublication manuscripts in one fully searchable database from publishers like O'Reilly Media, Prentice Hall Professional, Addison-Wesley Professional, Microsoft Press, Sams, Que, Peachpit Press, Focal Press, Cisco Press, John Wiley & Sons, Syngress, Morgan Kaufmann, IBM Redbooks, Packt, Adobe Press, FT Press, Apress, Manning, New Riders, McGraw-Hill, Jones & Bartlett, Course Technology, and dozens more. For more information about Safari Books Online, please visit us online.

How to Contact Us

Please address comments and questions concerning this book to the publisher:

O'Reilly Media, Inc.
1005 Gravenstein Highway North
Sebastopol, CA 95472
800-998-9938 (in the United States or Canada)
707-829-0515 (international or local)
707-829-0104 (fax)

We have a web page for this book, where we list errata, examples, and any additional information. You can access this page at *http://oreil.ly/comp_sci_basics_ruby*.

To comment or ask technical questions about this book, send email to *bookques tions@oreilly.com*.

For more information about our books, courses, conferences, and news, see our website at *http://www.oreilly.com*.

Find us on Facebook: *http://facebook.com/oreilly*

Follow us on Twitter: *http://twitter.com/oreillymedia*

Watch us on YouTube: *http://www.youtube.com/oreillymedia*

Acknowledgments

Gone are the days where one needs to set the stage with "computers are everywhere" or "computers are a commodity." Clearly, computers are everywhere, are used by everyone, and permeate every daily function and activity. Unfortunately, the majority of society can only use ready-made computer applications; they cannot *program* computers. With this book, we intend to change that!

In authoring this book, a five-year process, we benefited from and are grateful for the help of many; here we name but a few and apologize to those whose help we inadvertently forgot to acknowledge by name.

We thank all the students who persevered through the many instantiations of this text, from those who read the initial chapters over and over and over again as part of IIT's offerings. Their comments, suggestions, and criticisms guided our corrections through the iterations.

The entire production of this book, from the first partial drafts to the final version delivered to O'Reilly, was managed by two students, initially by Yacin Nadji (a doctoral student at Georgia Tech) and more recently by Andrew Yates (a doctoral student at Georgetown University). Without their help, we would have stumbled over one another, and we would have given up the effort many times over.

We use and envision others will use our book in the classroom. To aid instruction, we provide corresponding slides that would not exist without the help of two Georgetown University students, Candice Penelton and Sarah Chang.

We benefited from many editorial remarks; we thank the editorial changes suggested by Becca Page, the anonymous reviewers, and most notably, Mike Fitzgerald, who not only reviewed the book word by word, but also tested our code. We also thank Jason Soo for his periodic assistance with the Ruby source code and Abdur Chowdhury for his general guidance and assistance. Likewise, we thank the entire O'Reilly production team, who went way beyond what could be expected and significantly improved this book.

Finally and foremost, we thank our family members whose support and tolerance helped us through our jointly endured struggles (for David: Mary Catherine, Isaac, and Joseph; for Gideon: Dalia; and for Ophir: Nazli).

CHAPTER 1

Introduction to Computer Science

In This Chapter

- Defining computer science
- Programming techniques
- Algorithms and algorithm efficiency

1.1 Introduction

Introductory students often confuse programming with computer science, but programming is merely a strategy to implement computer science concepts. We introduce the basics of computer science using the Ruby programming language. Given our goal, we intentionally forgo many of the intricacies of the language.

Computer science is never tied to a programming language; it is tied to the task of solving problems efficiently using a computer. A computer comes with some resources, which will be discussed in Chapter 2, such as internal memory for short-term storage, processing capability, and long-term storage devices. A *complete program* is a set of instructions that use the computer to solve a real problem. The tool for producing these instructions is called a *programming language*. The goal is to develop solutions that use these resources efficiently to solve real problems.

Programming languages come and go, but the essence of computer science stays the same. If we need to sort a sequence of numbers, for example, it is immaterial if we sort them using programming language A or B. The steps the program will follow, commonly referred to as the *algorithm*, will remain the same. Hence, the core goal of computer science is to study algorithms that solve real problems. Computer scientists strive to create a correct sequence of steps that minimize resource demands, operate in a timely fashion, and yield correct results.

Algorithms are typically specified using pseudocode. Pseudocode, which may itself be simply written in plain language, specifies the logical, conceptual steps that must occur without specifying the necessary details needed to actually execute each step. However, we think that a properly selected subset of Ruby is sufficiently simple to introduce the algorithms. So, instead of creating an algorithm by writing it in plain language, generating equivalent pseudocode, and transforming it into a programming language, we go straight from the plain-language definition of an algorithm to Ruby code.

1.2 Application Development

When writing a program, it is important to keep in mind that the computer will do exactly what you tell it to do. It cannot think as a human would, so you must provide clear instructions for every step.

When giving instructions to others, people will often fill in blanks in logic without even realizing it. For example, if you instruct someone to "go to the bank," you may not say what mode of transportation should be used. A computer, however, does not have the ability to "fill in the blanks." A computer will only do exactly what you tell it to do.

Imagine, for example, explaining to a person and to a computer how to make a peanut butter and jelly sandwich. To the person, all you might need to say is, "Spread the peanut butter on one slice of bread, the jelly on the other slice of bread, and then put the pieces of bread together." If these instructions were given to a computer, however, the computer would not know where to start. Implied in these instructions are many logical steps that a human can automatically infer and the computer cannot. For example, the human would know that the jar must first be opened to scoop peanut butter out before you can spread it onto a slice of bread. The computer might try to spread the actual jar across the bread, without taking the peanut butter or jelly out—assuming it could even find them!

Computer science is ultimately about problem solving. The following is a basic approach to solving problems:

> Step 1: Understand the problem.
> Step 2: Write out a solution in plain language.
> Step 3: Translate the language into code.
> Step 4: Test the code in the computer.

Step 1: Understand the Problem

During this step, you try to answer all questions about the problem at hand. For example, you may be asked to create a program that stores a list of names, like a directory. Instead of just creating this program with little forethought, it is important to know all the details of the problem. Here are some examples:

- How many names will be stored?
- Do first and last names need to be stored separately?
- Are middle names needed?
- What is the maximum length that a name can be?

Step 2: Write Out the Solution in Plain Language

Once the problem is understood, the next step is to write an outline of how you will solve it. An example of the process of storing a name might look like a sequence of sentences:

Ask for the first name.

Store the first name.

Ask for the last name.

Store the last name.

Optionally, ask for the middle initial.

Store the middle initial.

Step 3: Translate the Language into Code

Once the plain-language version is written, it is time to translate it into actual code. The Ruby code for the preceding example is shown in Example 1-1, but you are certainly not expected to understand it yet.

Note the pound sign (#) on the righthand side. This sign means that the remainder of the line is a *comment*. A comment is not part of the instructions given to the computer. That is, a comment is a nonexecutable segment of code. Typically, comments are used to explain what the code does. Not only is it critical to comment code for the sake of readability and understanding, but using comments is considered good programming style, and the liberal use of comments is essential. Always remember that you (or someone else) may have to fix errors—colloquially referred to as bugs—years after you write a program; comments will help you understand what your code does years after you initially wrote it.

Gem of Wisdom

Algorithms are the core of computer science. Correct and efficient algorithms guarantee that the computer works smart rather than only hard. Thus, think about the problem, come up with a good algorithm, and then determine how many steps the computer needs to complete the task.

Example 1-1. Plain language → Ruby code

```
1 puts "Enter first name: " # Ask for the first name
2 first_name = gets  # Store the first name
3 puts "Enter last name: " # Ask for the last name
4 last_name = gets  # Store the last name
5 puts "Enter middle initial: " # Ask for the middle initial
6 middle_initial = gets  # Store the middle initial
```

Step 4: Test the Code in the Computer

This step entails running the program you created and seeing that it runs properly. It is best to test portions of your code as you write them, instead of writing an entire program only to find out that none of it works.

1.3 Algorithms

Algorithms are step-by-step methods of solving problems. The process of reading in names previously described is an example of an algorithm, though a very simple one. Some are extremely complicated, and many vary their execution depending on input. Often algorithms take input and generate output, but not always. However, all algorithms have something in common: they all do something.

Imagine a website like Google Maps, which has an algorithm to get directions from one point to another in either North America or Europe. It typically requires two inputs: a source and a destination. It also gives two outputs: the narrative directions to get from the source to the destination, and a map of the route.

The directions produced are also an algorithm; they accomplish the task of getting from the source to the destination. Imagine getting the directions to your friend's house shown on the map in Figure 1-1.

1. Start going south on River Road.
2. Turn left (east) on Main Street.
3. Take a right (south) on Ruby Lane.
4. Turn left (east) toward Algorithm Circle.
5. Continue until you come to 345 Algorithm Circle (your friend's house).

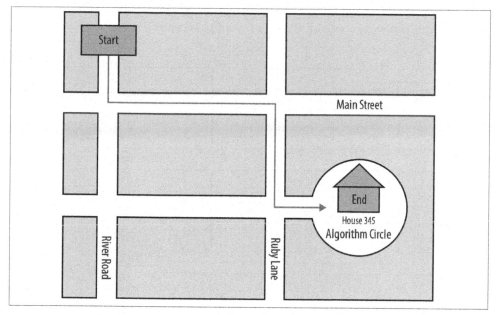

Figure 1-1. Directions "algorithm"

First notice that the directions are numbered; each step happens in sequential order. Additionally, it describes general steps like, "Turn left (east) on Main Street." It does not say, "Turn on your left turn signal and wait for the light to turn green, and then turn left on Main Street." That is not the point of an algorithm. An algorithm does not need to write out every single detail, but it needs to have all the important parts.

1.3.1 Algorithm Efficiency

Different algorithms may accomplish the same task, but some will do it much faster than others. Consider the algorithm just described for going to your friend's house, which certainly is not the only route to her or his home. Instead of getting on Ruby Lane, you could have hopped on the expressway, gone to the airport, and then taken a cab from the airport to your friend's house—but that would be extremely inefficient. Likewise, there may be a more efficient route to your friend's house than the one described. Just because you have created an algorithm does not make it efficient, and being able to create efficient algorithms is one of the factors that distinguishes a good computer scientist. For example, imagine receiving the following set of directions to your friend's house instead of the ones shown in the previous section, illustrated on the map in Figure 1-2:

1. Start going south on River Road.

2. Turn left (east) one block south of Main Street onto Algorithm Circle.

3. Continue until you come to 345 Algorithm Circle (your friend's house).

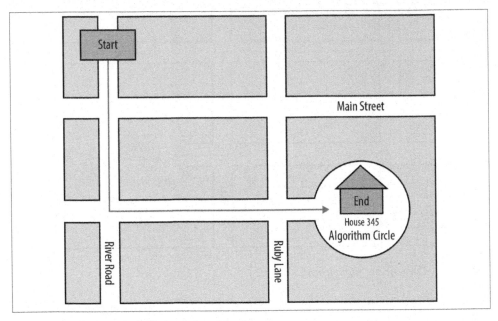

Figure 1-2. Directions "efficient algorithm"

Here we use a different algorithm that accomplishes the same task, and it does so slightly more efficiently. That is, fewer turns are involved.

1.4 Summary

You now understand the core foundations of computer science, namely the use of algorithms to solve real-world problems. Ruby, as used throughout the remainder of the book, is a powerful, yet relatively easy to understand, programming language that can be used to implement these algorithms. It is, however, critical to remember that independent of the programming language used, without a good algorithm, your solution will be ineffective.

1.4.1 Key Concepts

- The essence of computer science is problem solving. Computer science involves using the computer as a tool to model or solve various problems, from storing names in a database to finding efficient directions to a friend's house.

Gem of Wisdom

Once we have an algorithm, we can compare it to other algorithms and pick the best one for the job. Once the algorithm is done, we can write a program to implement it.

- When programming, it is important to understand that the computer is never wrong. It is merely following the directions you have given it.
- The following are basic steps for solving a computer science problem:

  Step 1: Understand the problem.
  Step 2: Write out a solution in plain language.
  Step 3: Translate the language into code.
  Step 4: Test the code in the computer.

- Algorithms are step-by-step methods for solving problems. When writing an algorithm, it is important to keep in mind the algorithm's efficiency.

1.4.2 Key Definitions

- *Algorithm*: A step-by-step method for solving problems.
- *Algorithm efficiency*: A measurement that determines how efficient one algorithm is compared with another.

1.5 Exercises

1. Imagine that you are creating a pocket calculator. You have created the functionality for all the buttons except x^2, the button that squares a number, and *exp*, which allows you to calculate base^{exponent}, where *exponent* is an integer. You may use any other functionality a calculator would normally have: for example, (+, -, *, /, =).

   a. Create the functionality for the x^2 button.

   b. Create the functionality for the *exp* button.

2. In the third-grade math class of French mathematician Carl Gauss, the teacher needed to give the students some busywork. She asked the class to compute the sum of the first 100 numbers (1 to 100). Long before the rest of the class had finished. Carl raised his hand and told his teacher that he had the answer: 5,050.

a. Craft an algorithm that will sum the first n numbers (assuming $n \geq 1$). How many steps does your algorithm take to complete when $n = 100$? How many steps does it take when $n = 1,000$?

b. Can you create an algorithm like Gauss's where the number of steps does not depend on n?

3. A palindrome is a word or phrase that reads the same way forward and backward, like "racecar." Describe a sequence of steps that determines if a word or phrase is a palindrome.

4. Consider the three mazes shown in Figure 1-3. Describe two different algorithms for solving a maze. Discuss advantages and disadvantages of each algorithm. Then look at the maze and predict which algorithm will complete first. See if your predictions were correct by applying your algorithms to the mazes.

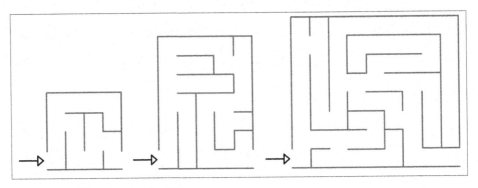

Figure 1-3. Three mazes for Exercise 4

5. Figure 1-4 shows an alternative way to represent an algorithm. (Note: we introduce this construct in detail later on. If it looks too intimidating, skip it until after you've read Chapter 4.)

a. Starting at the circle labeled "Start" work your way through the figure. What is the purpose of this algorithm?

b. Translate the figure into simple language. Note that a diamond in the figure represents a condition that may be true or false.

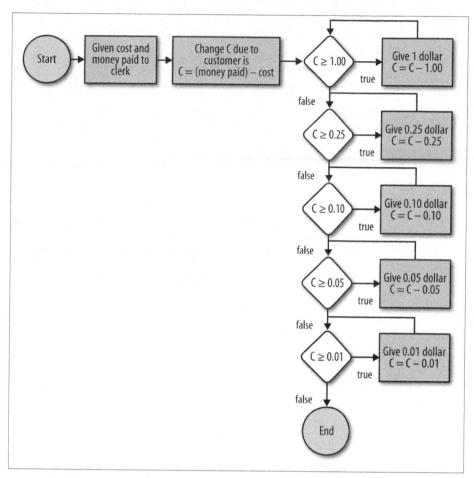

Figure 1-4. Alternative representation of an algorithm for Exercise 5

6. A cable company must use cables to connect 15 homes together so that every home is reachable by every other home. The company has estimated the costs of different cable routes (Figure 1-5 shows the numbers associated with each link). One engineer provides an algorithm, shown in Figure 1-5, that will find the cheapest set of routes to pick. Does the engineer's algorithm work for this case? Why or why not?

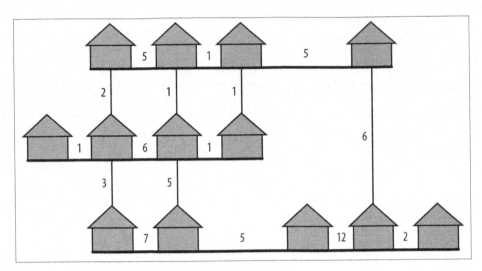

Figure 1-5. Cable company dilemma for Exercise 6

Engineer's Algorithm:

a. Pick one cable route with the lowest cost not already picked. Add this route to the set of cheapest routes.

b. Check if every house is connected to every other house through any series of cables. If it isn't, go back to step 1. If every house is connected, then the cheapest set of routes has been found.

CHAPTER 2

How Does the Computer Really Work?

In This Chapter

- Basic nomenclature and components of a computer system
- Bit strings and their meaning

2.1 Introduction

This book is about the basics of computer science in which algorithms are expressed by software; it is not about computer hardware. However, as software is the tool by which we use the computer, a rudimentary knowledge of the properties of computers is desirable to understand the attributes, properties, limitations, and sometimes idiosyncrasies, of software.

2.2 Basic Nomenclature and Components of a Computer System

It may be argued that this brief introduction to hardware is unnecessary. The computer has become a utilitarian device, to be used by people who are nontechnical—the same way that a car can be used by all people, without any need to understand the workings of the engine, the various support systems, and the energy management of the car. This is true, but only partially.

Consider a hybrid car, such as the Toyota Prius. It is designed to be just like any other car: drivable without the intricate understanding needed to grasp the concept of the synergy drive of a car where multiple modes of propulsion cooperate to optimize the energy usage of this essentially electric car. However, the actual energy consumption differs between drivers. Those who understand the working of this car will get better energy efficiency than the casual driver—in our experience sometimes as high as a 15% difference.

We argue that the same concept is true for software. Understanding the underlying machinery (the computer system) enables more efficient software development. This may not be important for small tasks, but it may be crucial for very large ones.

A *digital computer*—and we limit ourselves to these only—is a device that has three main parts: at least one processing unit, called the central processing unit or CPU, at least one memory unit, and a control unit. A *computer system* has, in addition to a computer, a set of peripheral devices that can be roughly divided into three categories: user interface devices, mass storage devices, and communication devices.

Most of the computers today are based on the Von Neumann model of computing, which is as follows: the memory holds computer programs and all the data values that are necessary for the computer program. A *computer program* is built from instructions that are executed in a logical sequence. The computer operates by causing the control unit to select an instruction from memory. That instruction causes the control unit to fetch data from the memory to the processing unit. There may be one data item, more than one, or none. The processing unit then performs the function implied by the instruction, and the control unit saves the result in memory and selects the next instruction to be fetched from memory.

This is the gist of the Von Neumann model. In reality, there are various types of memory, very complex control units, and optionally multiple processing units that can deal with many instructions in parallel. There are many other optimizations, but no matter how complex, logically, there is a strict serialization imposed by this model, and the instructions seem to be performing serially.

The memory stores all its contents, be it instructions or data, as numbers. The representation of numbers that we use is called the *radix* or positional representation. To create such a representation, we choose a radix (sometimes called the *base*) of the representation, say, r. We select r symbols that have the values of 0 through $r - 1$. Numbers are then represented by a sequence of these symbols. Each position in the sequence has an ordinal (sequence position number), counted from right to left. Thus, the rightmost position has the ordinal 0, the next one has ordinal 1, and so on. The value of the represented number is then computed by multiplying the value of the symbol in position n by the weight or the factor of that position, that is, r^n, and adding all values together.

In our familiar decimal system, the radix is 10. The 10 symbols that we use are 0, 1, 2, 3, 4, 5, 6, 7, 8, and 9. We call these symbols digits, carrying the values from zero to $r - 1$ which is 9. For example, to see what is represented by a three-digit number, say, 123, we compute the weight of each position. Position 0 will have the factor 10^0, which is 1,

Gem of Wisdom

A computer system has two types of memory: short-term random access memory (RAM) that is fast but limited (usually measured in gigabytes with access times in nanoseconds) and long-term that is thousands of times slower but far more vast (often measured in terabytes with access times in milliseconds). Additionally, a computer has a few small brains or central processing units (CPUs) that execute instructions, input and output mediums, and a network connection to support the exchange of information between machines.

the second position has the factor 10^1, which is 10, and the third has the factor 10^2, which is 100. The value of the number is thus $3 \times 1 + 2 \times 10 + 1 \times 100 = 123$, as expected.

Assume now radix 4—that is, the base of our positional system is 4, usually called the quaternary system. We need four symbols that we choose to be 0, 1, 2, and 3, with the obvious values. These are our quaternary numerals.

What is the (decimal) value of our three-digit number 123_4, where the subscript denotes that it is in base 4? The positions now have weights (factors) of $4^0 = 1$, $4^1 = 4$, and $4^2 = 16$. The decimal value of our number is now $3 \times 1 + 2 \times 4 + 1 \times 16$, which is, in decimal, 27.

Another quaternary system, used heavily in genetics, uses the symbols A, C, G, and T, expressing the sequence of DNA nucleotides (A C G T) as a quaternary number, sometimes using its decimal value.

The prevalent numerical form used in our computers is based on the radix 2, and is called binary. In the binary system, every binary digit, called a bit, has one of two possible values, 0 or 1. The number stored in the memory is thus composed from a string of bits, each having a value of zero or one. The meaning of the string is decided by the way it is used; it may be interpreted in many ways, to be discussed later in this chapter.

Memory is built from cells, and each cell has its own unique address. Most computers use consecutive natural numbers, starting from zero, as addresses, sometimes called locations. In most computers, the addresses refer to cells that can hold eight bits—we refer to these cells as *bytes*. These bytes can be accessed in an arbitrary order, that is, the computer can select any address to read from or write into. For this reason, these memories are referred to as random access memories or RAM.

Bytes can be grouped into larger strings and accessed as an ordered string of bits, as will be apparent throughout this book. Modern computers have memories that hold billions of bytes (we will discuss sizes in the following section).

The peripheral devices that complement the computer to create a computer system are, as already mentioned, of three different categories. We sometimes also subdivide each category into input (to the computer), output (from the computer), or input/output or I/O devices.

The user interface devices used for input are, for example, keyboards, touch screens, microphones, and various sensors. Examples of output devices in this category are printers, screens, drawing and typing devices, light and audio devices, and various signaling devices.

Mass storage devices are designed to hold information many orders of magnitude larger than memories. They include various types of magnetic devices, such as disks, tapes, and memory cards, optical devices such as CD or DVD drives, and electromagnetic devices such as mass memories. Almost all of these fall in the I/O category, although many may be input only, such as nonwritable CDs and DVDs or read-only memories (referred to as ROM). The properties of all these devices are dramatically different from RAM.

The development of new manufacturing technologies that enable large, low-power-consumption, solid-state memories, and the parallel development of novel, high-capacity batteries, is creating a shift in the structure of computer systems. The new solid-state memories are slowly replacing the traditional, magnetic-memory-based, mechanically powered disks and the optically based CD and DVD memory devices. As of 2012, tablets, mobile devices, and even laptop computers have no mechanical components, and thus no disk, DVD, or CD devices; all such devices are replaced by solid-state large memories. There are, however, external disk, CD, and DVD drives that can be connected to these new computing devices, thus providing both a transition path and backup capabilities for the computing devices. These drives are powered through the computer system itself (via their data connection interface—currently the USB); therefore, they do not require power connections of their own.

Communication devices are typically I/O devices that connect the computer to a network, be it local in a room, or global. These may be without a physical connecting device (wireless, line-of-sight microwave, light of various spectrum, sound wave activator, or sensor) or wired (copper cable, fiber optics, or sound conduit).

The peripheral devices are controlled by the I/O part of the control unit and require quite a sophisticated set of software programs to make them useful. The reader is referred to any basic book about operating systems to complement her or his knowledge of this subject. For a list of suggested reading, see Appendix A.

2.3 Scales of Magnitude

Mass storage devices and memories are very large and thus measured with units that have names different from those used in everyday life. While we use the colloquial word *grand* to refer to $1,000, for amounts greater than $1,000 we use the names of the decimal system, such as *million*. These are not universally used—in the United States, one thousand million is called *billion*; in Europe it is called *milliard*. There is, however, an agreed upon nomenclature for powers of 10 so that one thousand is called *kilo*, one million is called *Mega*, and so on (see Table 2-1). Note the lowercase in kilo, the uppercase in Mega, and all that follow. This comes from the fact that the letter *K* is reserved, in the decimal nomenclature, for the designation of the absolute temperature measure (degrees in Kelvin).[1]

Table 2-1. Scales of magnitude

Units	Actual size (bytes)	Other names	Real-world quantities
Megabyte (MB)	1,000,000	Million, 10^6	The King James version of the Bible contains approximately 5 million characters.
Mebibyte (MiB)	1,048,576	2^{20}	The speed of light is 300 million meters/second.
Gigabyte (GB)	1,000,000,000	Billion, 10^9	At 5% interest, $1 billion would return $50,000,000/year.
Gibibyte (GiB)	1,073,741,824	2^{30}	A billion $1 bills, end to end, would wrap the Earth at the equator 4.5 times.
Terabyte (TB)	1,000,000,000,000	Trillion, 10^{12}	The U.S. GDP for 2006 was $13 trillion.
Tebibyte (TiB)	1,099,511,627,776	2^{40}	Global GDP in 2006 was estimated by the World Bank to be $46 trillion.
Petabyte (PB)	1,000,000,000,000,000	Quadrillion, 10^{15}	108×10^{15} meters is the distance to the nearest star (excluding the sun), Alpha Centauri.
Pebibyte (PiB)	2^{50}		Large multinational enterprises and massive scientific databases are in this neighborhood of storage.
Exabyte (EB)	10^{18}	Quintillion	The oceans on the Earth contain about 326 quintillion gallons of water.
Exbibyte (EiB)	2^{60}		
Zettabyte (ZB)	10^{21}	Sextillion	
Zebibyte (ZiB)	2^{70}		

The computer is not based on the radix 10; it is based on the radix 2. Inasmuch as 2^{10} equals 1,024, which is close to 10^3, it became customary in the past to refer to 2^{10} as *kilo*. Thus, one kilobyte was approximately one thousand bytes, and the discrepancy was small. When we move from a kilobyte to a megabyte, which now stands for 2^{20} bytes, the discrepancy between 10^6 and 2^{20} is significant, as $10^6 = 1,000,000$ and $2^{20} = 1,048,576$. This is not a small difference and cannot be ignored. Obviously, as we move toward larger scales, the discrepancy in sizes expressed as decimal names for binary-based quantities is increased, causing confusion and inconsistency in reporting sizes.

For that reason, as of 2005, there is a standard that introduces new names for quantities expressed as powers of 2 and retains the familiar names for quantities expressed as powers of 10. Table 2-1 has names, sizes, and observations about the real meaning of

---

1. *http://en.wikipedia.org/wiki/Kelvin*

the sizes, starting with megabyte for the decimal meaning of the size in bytes and mebibytes for the binary meaning. As of the time of this writing (2013), sizes of mass storage devices are usually quoted in the decimal meanings, and sizes of RAM are quoted in the binary meaning, both using the decimal nomenclature. This confusion, well exploited in advertising, will hopefully disappear as the binary nomenclature becomes better used, or if the community will decide to report correctly when decimal nomenclature is used.

Please refer to Table 2-1 to make sense of what you just read. The binary prefixes were first proposed by the IEC (International Electrotechnical Commission) in January 1999 and expanded in 2005 to include all binary equivalents to the accepted decimal prefixes. All binary prefixes and names were codified by the IEEE (Institute of Electrical and Electronics Engineers) as a standard in 2005 (IEEE 1541-2002).

2.4 Instruction Execution—Speed and Timing Scales

As explained earlier, programs operate by the control unit causing the central processing unit to execute instructions in a logically sequential manner. It is immaterial how many instructions are in a different execution phase at any point in time; their effect is transmitted in a serial fashion, one instruction at a time.

Instructions are executed in phases that take time, each controlled by a timing mechanism called a clock. In reality, there may be several clocks, but suffice it to say that clocks operate in various frequencies that define the basic time step of the instruction execution phases. Clock speeds are measured in Hertz (Hz), where 1 Hz is one clock cycle per second.

The scales of time and frequency are summarized in Table 2-2. It is important to realize the meaning of the scales represented there.

Modern computers (in 2013) operate on a clock that is typically somewhere between 2 GHz and 1 THz. The way that clock speed translates into instructions executed per second is not trivial and depends heavily on the design and cost of the computer. Again, that is not the topic of this book. Here we just state that while there is a link between the clock speed and the instruction execution rate, it should not be inferred that computer A with a clock rate double that of computer B will perform at twice the speed of B. The complication arises partially from overlap between phases of instruction execution and from the fact that different instructions typically take a different number of clock steps to execute.

To get a better handle on computer speeds, we measure them by the instruction rate rather than the time each instruction takes. These ratings are sometimes expressed in MIPS (Millions of Instructions Per Second) or FLOPS (FLoating-point Operations Per Second), and by multiples of these units such as MegaFLOPS or TeraFLOPS. To determine computer speeds, specially crafted programs are run and their execution times are recorded. This measures speed more realistically than simply using the processor's clock speed.

Table 2-2. Scales of time and frequency

Units	Fraction of a second	Symbol	Real-world quantities
Second	1	sec	The speed of light is 300 million meters/sec.
Hertz	1	Hz	
Millisecond	10^{-3}	msec	A high-speed disk rotates once in 10 msec.
Kilohertz	10^3	KHz	
Microsecond	10^{-6}	μsec	A typical laptop performs about 8,000 basic instructions in about one microsecond (Intel Core 2 Duo).
Megahertz	10^6	MHz	
Nanosecond	10^{-9}	nsec	Light traverses only 30 cm in one nanosecond.
Gigahertz	10^9	GHz	An instruction on a computer is done in several nanoseconds.
Picosecond	10^{-12}	psec	
Terahertz	10^{12}	THz	
Femtosecond	10^{-15}	fsec	

As supercomputers increase in size and speed, the complexity of problems solved by them increases to a point that the access of data in memory dominates the speed of execution. This necessitates new approaches to speed evaluations. As an example, one of the newer approaches (in 2011) introduced a measure called gigateps, a billion traversed edges per second, based on the speed of solving an analysis of the connections, or edges, between points in a graph.

Timing considerations are important not only for instruction execution, but also for the operation of peripheral devices and communication devices. These considerations, as with the previous ones relating to instruction speed, are beyond the scope of this book. Suffice it to say that the rotational speed of disks, measured in microseconds, is many orders of magnitude slower than the execution rate of instructions. Significant portions of operating systems are devoted to mitigate this difference so that the speed of execution will be minimally impacted by the slowness of the peripheral devices.

2.5 Bit Strings and Their Meaning

As discussed before, the contents of the memory consist of strings of bits. Most computers have these stored in individually addressable units of eight bits, called *bytes*. The bytes in turn can be strung together to form longer strings. For historical reasons, a group of two consecutive bytes is called a *half word*, four bytes (32 bits) are called a *word*, and 64 bytes are called a *double* or *long word*.

The meaning of the strings of bits is just that—a string of bits. The interpretation of the meaning, however, is dependent on the usage of the string. One important usage is to code an instruction and its parameters. There are many types of instructions: numerical, like add and multiply, logical, control, program flow, and others. Again, this book is not devoted to hardware details, so we do not elaborate. Simply said, a string of bits can be interpreted as an instruction, and given the address of the proper byte in this string, the control unit will try to decode and execute that instruction. The instruction itself will cause the control unit to find the next instruction, and so on.

Bit strings also can represent data. Here we have a wide variety of possibilities, so we restrict ourselves to the most prevalent data coding.

The simplest one is the integer. In this interpretation, the bit string represents a positive numerical value in radix 2. This means that each string represents a binary number, where each digit is weighed by the proper power of two, starting from zero on the extreme right (end of the string) and proceeding to the left. Thus, the string 01011101 will have the meaning $1 \times 2^0 + 0 \times 2^1 + 1 \times 2^2 + 1 \times 2^3 + 1 \times 2^4 + 0 \times 2^5 + 1 \times 2^6 + 0 \times 2^7$, where $\times$ is the multiplication sign. Evaluating this expression, the string 01011101 has the value of $1 + 0 + 4 + 8 + 16 + 0 + 64 + 0$ or 93. We do not discuss here how negative values are represented, but they are available.

Integer values are limited by the length of their string representations. Ruby recognizes two types of integers: regular and long. We discuss those (and other numeric representations) and their properties in a forthcoming chapter.

To alleviate the limitation of size imposed on integers, a very important representation of data is available. It is called *floating point* or *real*. The former name is older and used primarily in discussing hardware concepts.

In this interpretation, numbers are represented in scientific form, that is, as $x \times 2^y$. Thus, part of the string is used to hold the value of x and part is used to hold the value of y. Both x and y are expressed by their binary values, derived in the same way that we presented in our discussion of integers, or in a complex form as negative values introduce additional difficulties. As you will see, there are different types of real numbers.

The last interpretation that we discuss is that of characters.

Character representation follows an international standard, codified under the name Unicode. The standard provides for a representation of both character and noncharacter-based texts (such as, for example, Far East languages) and for the representation of other items (such as, for example, mathematical symbols, control characters, etc.). The Unicode representation uses one to four bytes per item. The first 256 characters, digits, symbols, and codes are contained in one byte and are identical to the previous standard known as ASCII (American Standard for Character Information Interchange). Almost all English-based texts files belong to this category, so it is customary to state that characters are single bytes.

Gem of Wisdom

Programs in Ruby or any other programming language are strictly human-readable. However, a computer only understands only instructions that are encoded as a sequence of 1s and 0s (binary digits). Thus, we use another program called an interpreter (done one step at a time) or a compiler (done for all steps) that translates the English-like programming language to binary machine instruction codes.

For in-depth information on this important topic, the voluminous Unicode standard description (currently more than 600 pages) contains tables, descriptions, rules, and explanations for dozens of different scripts, languages, symbols, and so on.

There is a difference between character representations and their meaning. For example, the character "9" is *not* the number 9. The number 9 is represented by the character "9." This distinction will be very important in future chapters as we have input programs that read characters, but we wish to use them as numbers. In our former example, we have seen that the number 93 is stored as the string 01011101, but the character string "93" will be stored in a completely different way. To obtain the number 93 from the character string "93," we need a process of conversion from the character to the numerical representation. Ruby provides such a process, as do all programming languages.

These are the most important but by no means the only types of interpretations of bit strings. Some others may represent different types of data, be they components of colors for the display, controls for various devices, amplitudes for sound presentation, and so on.

2.6 The Interpreter Process and Ruby

We now have covered the general concepts of computer systems embodied in a Von Neumann–style machine. We stated that programs and the data used by them reside in central memory, which can be replenished by various peripheral devices. We also stated that the memory stores its content in bits—binary digits consisting of 1's and 0's.

In the following chapters we will introduce various algorithms or processes designed to solve problems. Among all possible ways to introduce and express the algorithms, we have chosen the Ruby programming language. This language, and other programming languages, express the algorithms via sequences of unambiguous sentences called *statements*. These are written using the Latin character set, digits in decimal notation, and special symbols, such as =, , , >, and others. Clearly, these are not binary digits, so these are not programs that can be directly executed by a computer. What procedure is used to accept programs written in a language like Ruby and causes them to be performed or, as we say, executed, by a computer?

There are several methods to accomplish this task. We will dwell on two of these: *compilation* and *interpretation*. In the interpretation process, we will use two different approaches, so one can claim that we will introduce three methods.

To begin, we will assume that the program to be executed is contained in a file produced, say, by a word processor such as Microsoft Word or a similar one. As a matter of fact, in this book we will advocate using a word processor that is directly geared toward writing Ruby programs, as opposed to a general-purpose word processor.

It is important to bear in mind that this book does not intend to cover the areas of compilation and interpretation. All we do here is introduce the concepts so that the rest of this book will be better understood.

Compilation is a process that analyzes a program statement by statement, and for each statement produces the instructions that execute the algorithm steps implied by that statement. Once all the statements are analyzed and the instructions produced, the compilation process will create a file containing the executable code for that program. That file, in turn, is loaded into the memory to be executed.

The compilation process is performed by a program called a *compiler*. Simply put, a compiler translates instructions written in a given computer language, call it X, to a format that can execute on a particular computer type, call it Y. Examples of X include C++, Java, and Ruby. Examples of Y include Intel's Core 2, Motorola's 68060, and NEC's V20. So formally, a compiler for language X for a computer Y is typically (but not always) a program that is written in instructions executable on Y and, while executing and residing in the memory of Y, accepts as input a file containing statements in the language X and producing a file containing instructions for execution on computer Y.

A modern computer system will typically have several compilers for several languages.

Interpretation is a horse of a different color. In this process, statements are analyzed one by one and executed as they are encountered. In the pure case of interpretation (there are variants not discussed here) *no* instructions for the computer are produced—only the effect of the statements is evident. There is, therefore, a program called an *interpreter* for language X (written for computer Y) that accepts, as input, statements in language X and executes them.

There are essentially two main ways to do interpretation, and both are supported by the Ruby interpreter. The first one is called the *interactive mode*. In this mode, the programmer is prompted by the interpreter to enter one statement at a time, and the interpreter executes it. It can be viewed as a glorified calculator. It is very useful for such tasks as short programs, concept evaluation, and experimenting with options. It also is a good way to check and see if a statement does what you think it will do. It is often a good idea to try something out in the interactive interpreter before you put it in a program.

The second mode is the so-called *batch mode* (the name has historical roots; do not worry about what it means). In this mode, the program is prepared the same way it is in compilation; it is prepared in its entirety and stored in a file. The file containing the program is used as the input to the interpreter that analyzes the file statement by statement and executes the statements one by one.

Ruby is an interpretive language. It is beyond the scope of this book to say more on this subject, but as you dive into the language, and in particular as you run programs, how it all works will become increasingly evident.

2.7 Summary

While algorithm design typically abstracts away the underlying target computer architecture, completely ignoring architecture in introductory computer science books unnecessarily limits the understanding of readers. Understanding computer architecture basics and accounting for such basics in the design of algorithms often reduces the running time of the algorithm on the target computer. Thus, in this chapter, the fundamental aspects of computer architecture were introduced. We described the basic components of a computer, the fundamentals of data representation, and various unit determinations.

2.7.1 Key Concepts

- The Von Neumann model of computing is the prevalent model in the architecture (structure) of computers, the one followed in this book.

- A computer consists of a single or several central processing unit(s), memory(ies), and a control unit.

- Both instructions and data reside in the memory.

- Instructions are followed in a sequential manner, with some instructions capable of causing changes in the sequence.

- A computer system includes a computer and peripheral devices of various types.

- Peripheral devices, sometimes called input/output devices, are divided into user/computer interface (including sensors), communication, and mass memory devices.

- All data are stored in binary form, but the interpretation of those data depends on their usage.

- Two means to execute instructions are compilation and interpretation.

2.7.2 Key Definitions

- *Central Processing Unit (CPU)*: The part of a computer that executes instructions.
- *Random Access Memory (RAM)*: The main memory of the computer (there are also RAM units available as peripheral devices). RAM contents can be modified.
- *Read-Only Memory (ROM)*: Memory whose contents cannot be modified by computer instructions.
- *Radix (base)*: The base of a positional system.
- *Integer*: Interpretation of memory contents as a whole number of limited range.
- *Real (floating-point) number*: Interpretation of memory contents as containing two parts, man (mantissa) and exp (exponent), so that the number is expressed as $man \times 2^{exp}$.
- *Character*: Interpretation of memory contents as a literal (letter, number, symbol, etc.).
- *Compilation*: Translation of instructions written in a given language to the language of instruction for the target machine.
- *Interpretation*: Step-by-step execution of the specified instructions.

2.8 Exercises

1. Write 208 in binary and in ternary (base 3). Hint: what are the ternary digits?

2. The octal system (base 8) uses the digits 0 through 7. The representation of the letter *A* in the ASCII encoding scheme is 1000001 in binary. What is it in octal?

3. Color pictures are built of pixels, each represented by three bytes of information. Each byte represents the intensity of the primary colors red, green, and blue (or RGB values). How many gigabytes of storage are required for a 1028×1028–pixel color picture?

4. A communication device has the capacity to transfer one megabit of data per second. A 90-minute movie is recorded at 25 frames per second, each frame consisting of 720×600 pixels. How long would it take to transfer this movie across the previously described communication device? Would someone be able to stream the video over this communication device without experiencing jittery playback? Explain why or why not.

CHAPTER 3

Core Programming Elements

In This Chapter

- How to install Ruby and save files
- Defining variables
- Data classes (types):
  — Integer
  — Float
  — String
  — Boolean
- Input and output
- Common programming errors

3.1 Introduction

The first chapter introduced computer science basics, focusing on the concept of algorithms. The second chapter discussed the basic components of a computer. Now it is time to introduce core programming elements, the most basic tools of programming languages. We will show examples of this using the Ruby programming language. These include constants and variables of various data types and the process of input and output. Also, we will explain common programming errors encountered when using the information covered in this chapter.

Gem of Wisdom

Plain text files (sometimes seen with the extension *.txt*) are stored as a simple sequence of characters in memory. For example, files created with Notepad on Windows are plain text files. Try to open a Microsoft Word document in Notepad and observe the results. Non-plain text files are commonly called *binary files*.

3.2 Getting Started

How to Install Ruby

The time has come for you to begin writing simple programs. Before you can do that, you need to install Ruby. This is explained in Appendix B at the back of the book.

How to Save Programs

The next thing to learn is how to save your work. When writing a computer program (informally called *code*), it is often important to be able to save it as a plain text file, which can be opened and used later.

To save a program, you must first open a piece of software that allows you to create, save, and edit text files. These programs are called *text editors*, and examples include Notepad, Scite (included in the one-click installation of Ruby), and many others we discuss in Appendix C. For more advanced editors, you may want to look into vim and emacs. There is also a version of the integrated development environment (IDE) Eclipse that works with Ruby. Eclipse includes a plain text editor. Once a text editor is open, be sure it is set to save as an unformatted text file (*FileName.txt*). Most word processors, such as Word, add special characters for document formatting, so these should not be used for writing programs. If special characters are turned off by saving the document as a plain text file (*.txt*), you can use various word processing programs, such as Word.

Now you are ready to write and save programs.

3.3 What Is a Variable?

A *variable* is a piece of data attached to a name. In algebra, a variable like x in the equation $x = y + 2$ indicates that x and y can take on many different values. In most programming languages, variables are defined just as in algebra and can be assigned different values at different times. In a computer, they refer to a location in memory. Although this is a simple concept, variables are the heart of almost every program you write. The Pythagorean theorem is shown in Figure 3-1, and it uses three variables: *A*, *B*, and *C*.

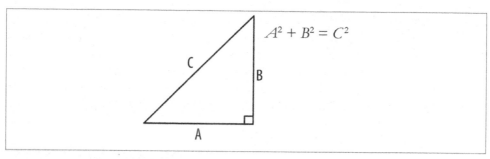

Figure 3-1. Pythagorean theorem

A, *B*, and *C* are the variable names, and they each represent a number. To create a variable in Ruby, simply use the format *variable_name = value*, where *variable_name* is the name of your variable and *value* is the value you would like it to have. The equal sign (=) behaves differently in Ruby from the way it does in algebra. In Ruby, = means "assign the RHS (righthand side) to the variables in the (LHS) lefthand side." The code snippet y = x + 2 means compute the value of x + 2 and store the result into the variable y. In algebra, *y = x + 2* simply explains a relationship between variables *x* and *y*.

An easy way to test things in Ruby is with *irb* (once Ruby is properly installed), the Interactive Ruby Shell. Enter irb from a command prompt; you can see that it is very easy to create variables. The following example shows several variables being created and assigned values.

```
irb(main):001:0> a = 4
=> 4
irb(main):002:0> b = 3
=> 3
irb(main):003:0> c = 5
=> 5
```

This example creates three variables named *a*, *b*, and *c* and initializes their data to 4, 3, and 5, respectively. While these variables were given simple names, variables can be given almost any name you wish. However, it is poor style to create variable names that are unclear (e.g., *x1, x2, zxy*). Variable names should explain the data they represent. When naming variables, avoid special characters (%, $, #, @, etc.) because these characters often carry specific meaning. Also note that variables cannot begin with integers. Ruby is case-sensitive, so myName is different from myname. Variable names should start with a lowercase letter, while constants (to be explained shortly) start with an uppercase letter. Additionally, people who write programs tend to be concerned about readability. Ruby users tend to name long variables with underscores (_). For example, instead of naming a variable primenumber or primeNumber, in Ruby it is named prime_number, although the former are both acceptable. This is simply a stylistic pattern, not a requirement.

A variable refers to a section of memory that has been set aside to hold whatever data you specify. Every location in memory has an address that can be accessed by a program. Instead of asking you to write a program to store the value *xx* into memory location *yy*, most programming languages allow you to identify a variable and assign a value to it. The picture in Figure 3-2 further illustrates the concept of variables and memory. `variable_1` has a value of 5 stored at location 10, while `variable_2` is stored at location 20 with a value of 8.

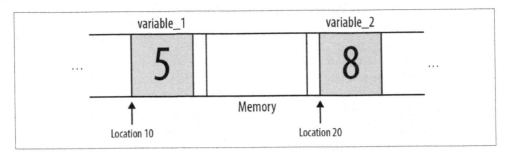

Figure 3-2. Memory diagram

Variables store different types of data, not just numbers. They can hold user-created data, words, numbers, and more. Depending on what type of data the variable is holding, it will have a different *data type*.

Constants: Variables That Never Change

If a variable does not change, it is called a *constant*. For example, 3.14159 is commonly understood as π or simply pi. By creating a variable called PI and never changing it, that is, making the variable into a constant, one can use PI throughout the program instead of repeatedly typing the numeral string. By following this convention, fewer errors are likely to occur as this value is only entered one time, namely when the constant value is assigned. Typing the value of π multiple times might lead to typing errors. Furthermore, readability is enhanced. For example, it is far more intuitive to describe an algorithm that computes the area of a circle as one that squares the radius and multiplies the result by PI than one that squares the radius and multiplies by 3.14159. As noted before, constant names start with a capital letter, and by convention are all uppercase.

Data Types

Data types indicate the nature of the variable and the range of valid values for that variable. Data types also indicate how much memory to allocate for each type of data. It is important to know that specific types of data have specific sizes in memory. As will be evident later, data types also define the meanings of allowed operators.

Gem of Wisdom

Ruby (along with many other programming languages) does not allow commas in numbers. Underscores, however, can be used in their place. Use an underscore in place of a comma if you need to mark your thousands so that larger numbers are more readable.

Ruby refers to data types as classes. In Ruby, as in other object-oriented languages, a class is a description of objects. A detailed discussion of objects takes place in Chapter 9. For now, the relevant Ruby classes are Fixnum, Bignum, Float, Boolean, and String.

Integer

An *integer* is defined as any natural number (0, 1, 2, . . .) or its negative (0, -1, -2, . . .). The integer data type is simply a subset of the infinite mathematical integers. In a 32-bit system, integers range in value from -2,147,483,648 to 2,147,483,647. Note that if the number of bits used differs, so will the range.

Consider the following:

```
irb(main):01:0> x = 5
=> 5
```

When we type in x = 5, we are doing two things. First, we are creating a variable x that stores an integer of the class Fixnum. Second, we are assigning the value of 5 to x. In some languages, variables must be explicitly assigned to a type before they are used. In Ruby, the class of the variable is either explicitly stated or inferred in every assignment of the variable. In this case, Ruby infers the Fixnum class.

Imagine creating a huge number, out of the range of supported integers:

```
irb(main):02:0> x = 1_000_000_000_000_000
=> 1000000000000000
```

The Bignum class is used by Ruby for very large integers not contained within the previously stated integer range. This class enables the creation of integers outside the range of those possible in Fixnum.

Float

Simply put, a *float* is a decimal number. In Ruby, floats can be defined either with numbers containing a decimal place or in scientific notation.

```
irb(main):001:0> x = 5.0
=> 5.0
irb(main):002:0> x = -3.14159
=> -3.14159
irb(main):003:0> x = 3.5e2
=> 350.0
```

Similar to the integers example, when we execute x = 3.14159, we create a variable x that stores a float. We then assign the value of 3.14159 to x. Negative values are expressed with a leading negative sign (-).

For scientific notation, values are expressed in powers of 10 following the symbol *e*. Hence, 3.5*e*2 indicates $3.5 \times 10^2 = 350$. Very small numbers can be represented as negative powers of 10. You may find that the designation *real* is used in other languages to denote *float*.

Strings

Strings are simply one or more characters surrounded by quotes. Both double quotes (") and single quotes (') can be used, but if you need to use a single quote inside your string, you must bound your string with double quotes (e.g., "The computer said, 'Hello World!' ").

```
irb(main):001:0> x = "hello world"
=> hello world
irb(main):002:0> y = "hello, 'world'"
=> hello, 'world'
```

To store characters (such as letters and symbols), a character encoding scheme, as discussed in Chapter 2, is used. For example, to encode the English alphabet, we need to represent 26 uppercase letters, 26 lowercase letters, and a variety of special characters. Using eight bits (one byte) per character allows us to encode 256 characters, a number more than sufficient to represent English. Each character is assigned a unique number from 0 to 255.

Booleans

Booleans can hold only two different values: true and false. They are sometimes referred to as *flags*.

```
irb(main):001:0> x = true
=> true
irb(main):002:0> y = false
=> false
```

3.4 Basic Arithmetic Operators

Now that some of the classes that define various data types have been introduced, what can you do with them? Like all other programming languages, Ruby is able to perform many mathematical operations. In Table 3-1, we illustrate how to use Ruby as a calculator.

Table 3-1. Basic arithmetic operators

Symbol	Operation	Example
+	Addition	x = 6 + 2 8
-	Subtraction	x = 3 - 2 1
*	Multiplication	x = 5 * 2 10
/	Division	x = 16/8 2
%	Modulus	x = 5 % 3 2
**	Power	x = 2 ** 4 16

All of the operators listed are binary operators, meaning the operator has two operands. For example, the command A + B is a binary operation, where A and B are the two operands and + is the operator.

When typing mathematical operations in the Ruby interpreter, the order of operations is taken into account. To change the order of operations, use parentheses. Try typing the following in the command line:

```
irb(main):001:0> x = 10 + 4 / 2
```

What result did you get? Now try entering the following into the prompt:

```
irb(main):001:0> x = (10 + 4) / 2
```

Most of the operators should look familiar. The one that might not is the modulus operator (%). The purpose of this operator is to find the remainder produced by dividing two numbers. For example, 4 modulo 2, abbreviated 4 mod 2, would produce the result 0. This is because 4 / 2 is exactly 2. On the other hand, 2 mod 4 produces a result of 2. This is because 2 / 4 is 0, with a remainder of 2. Let's try to solve a few easy problems using the modulus operator.

1. Using the mod operator, determine if a number is even. This should be fairly easy. We know that n is even if, when divided by 2, it produces a remainder of 0. So, if n mod 2 equals 0, then n is even.

   ```
   irb(main):001:0> x = 5%2
   => 1
   irb(main):002:0> x = 6%2
   => 0
   ```

2. Given a number as input, determine if the number is prime. That is, the given number must not have any factors other than 1 and itself. For example, 1, 3, 5, and

Gem of Wisdom

Components of a mathematical expression can usually be broken into operands and operators. For example, in the expression 2 + 3, 2 and 3 are operands, and + is the operator. Operands are usually values, and operators are the actions to be performed.

7 are prime numbers. The number 2 is the only even prime number since all other even numbers have 2 as a factor. Likewise, for example, the number 9 is also not prime since 3 divides it evenly. As an aside, finding prime numbers is one of the classic problems used to teach any programming language. Furthermore, prime numbers play a significant role in information security. For example, SSL (Secure Sockets Layer), which is what you use when you go to a website and type "https", uses an algorithm called public key encryption. This algorithm relies heavily on prime numbers. The intuition behind the use of prime numbers is that for long numbers (those that comprise hundreds of digits) it takes a computer a very long time to determine their factors. Thus, it is safe to publicly present these numbers.

Although we may not be able to program this yet, we can come up with an algorithm to solve this problem. Namely, we can do the following:

If n is equal to 2, then n is prime. Otherwise, take each number x in the range 2 to $n - 1$. If n mod x is equal to 0 for any of these numbers x, then the number n is not prime. If n mod x is not equal to 0 for every number in the range 2 to $n - 1$, then the number n is prime.

Note that this is not an efficient algorithm, but it is correct. Can you think of a more efficient approach? Hint: Do we really need to check all the way up to $n - 1$?

Now that we have discussed the basics, we will describe some slightly more advanced operations. Ruby has many built-in modules; a *module* is simply a *group of methods* for a particular domain. There are methods that accomplish many different tasks. We will discuss methods in great detail starting with Chapter 8. For example, Ruby has a built-in module for mathematics, the Math module. Table 3-2 lists some of the more advanced mathematical functions in Ruby. These functions are referred to as *methods*.

Table 3-2. Advanced arithmetic operations

Method	Operation	Example	Result
sqrt()	Square root	x = Math.sqrt(9)	3.0
sin()	Sine	x = Math.sin(0)	0.0
cos()	Cosine	x = Math.cos(0)	1.0
tan()	Tangent	x = Math.tan(0.7854)	1.0
log()	Natural log (ln)	x = Math.log(5)	1.609
log10()	Log (base 10)	x = Math.log10(10)	1.0

Gem of Wisdom

Ruby comes with many built-in functions called *methods* to make your life easier. Table 3-2 shows a few of them. Without a square root (i.e., sqrt()) function you would need to write a program to compute the square root by repeated division. For any programming language, make sure you learn about all the built-in functions, as they can save you significant time.

When trying to perform these operations, we specify the Math module, followed by a period (.), then the method (type of operation). For example, to find the square root of 16, type:

```
irb(main):001:0> x = Math.sqrt(16)
=> 4.0
```

To appreciate the power of the Math module and understand the order of operations in Ruby, try creating a program that performs the following operation:

$$x = \frac{5 + \sqrt{9}}{2}$$

The result should look similar to this:

```
irb(main):001:0> x = (5 + Math.sqrt(9)) / 2
=> 4.0
```

Make sure you obtain 4.0 as a result. If you do not, try again. With computers there is *no point in repeating failure* precisely. Often, novice programmers state: "Well, I tried it 500 times!" If no input was changed, rest assured that no output will change either. So *change something* and then try again! Be patient, check things carefully, and keep working until the result is 4.0. If you obtained 4.0 the first time, try some variations (e.g., misspell the word *Math*), and become familiar with some error messages. It is important to start being methodical about implementing programs on a computer on the very first day. Take your time, go slowly, and think about everything you enter. Sometimes with programming languages even the smallest detail can be the difference between success and failure.

3.5 Input and Output

Output Using Variables

Displaying text in Ruby is simple. Try entering the following at the command prompt:

```
irb(main):001:0> puts "Hello World"
```

The puts method (short for outPUT a String) simply displays a string on the screen. Notice the string is contained in quotation marks; otherwise, both Hello and World would be interpreted as variables. Variables are displayed on the screen using similar syntax, except without quotation marks:

```
irb(main):002:0> text = "Hello World"
=> "Hello World"
irb(main):003:0> puts text
=> Hello World
```

This example stores the string "Hello World" in a variable named text and then displays the value stored in the text variable using the puts method. This method is not limited to strings and can be used with other classes including integers, floats, and Booleans.

The use of classes to define data types means a variety of methods can be done for each type. For example, x.length indicates the size of a string when x is defined as a string.

Display User Input

Displaying user input in Ruby is almost as easy as displaying output. Try entering the following in the command prompt:

```
irb(main):001:0> age_input = gets
```

The gets method (short for GET a String from the user) stops the program and waits for the user to type some text and then press Enter. The text typed by the user will be stored as a string in a variable called age_input. Due to the nature of the gets method, the value stored in age_input will be a string, but you need an integer if you wish to mathematically manipulate it. We create another variable age and set it equal to the integer value of the user's input by converting the string age_input to an integer. This is done by issuing the following command:

```
irb(main):002:0> age = age_input.to_i
```

The method to_i converts age_input to an integer.

Basic Programs

Now that you have learned how to display text and request user input, you can develop a program that calculates the area of a rectangle. Try using the problem-solving approach discussed in Chapter 1 to create this program.

Step 1: Understanding the Problem

Ask yourself key questions that must be answered to properly design the program:

- How do you find the area of a rectangle?

- How many variables do you need to represent that area?
- What data type do the variables need to be?

Step 2: Write Out the Problem in Plain Language

Before writing out the problem, remember that the input method stores user input as strings, so we need to convert the lengths (which are stored as strings) to integers before performing mathematical operations with them.

1. Ask for the length.
2. Store the length.
3. Ask for the width.
4. Store the width.
5. Convert the length to an integer.
6. Convert the width to an integer.
7. Calculate rectangle area (area = length × width).
8. Display area.

The equation for the area of a rectangle is the product of its length and width. Although it does not affect this equation, remember that the rules for order of operations apply in Ruby. To change the order of operations, use parentheses.

Step 3: Rewrite the Plain Language into Code

See Example 3-1. In the figure, as with all other program illustrations, the line numbers are not part of the code; they are added strictly for explanatory purposes. In line 8, we are printing an integer represented in the variable `area`. This differs from the printing of character strings in lines 1 and 3. Ruby automatically determines the data type, if it can. This is called dynamic or "duck" typing. This functionality is helpful; however, as you will see, automatic type determination can introduce problems. In this example, though, it helps in that `puts area` is mapped to `puts area.to_s`. Note that generally speaking, the `.to_*` method is a type conversion operation where the target type is represented by the `*` (a wildcard). For example, you have now seen conversion to integer (`to_i`) and to string (`to_s`).

Gem of Wisdom

When you get an error message, do not just try the program again. This may work with your toaster, where you just unplug it and plug it back in, but with software development, it rarely, if ever, works. Figure out the problem, make a correction, and then see if it works.

Example 3-1. Code with comments

```
1 puts "What is the length?" # Ask for the length
2 length_input = gets  # Stores the length
3 puts "What is the width?" # Ask for the width
4 width_input = gets  # Stores the width
5 length  = length_input.to_i # Convert length to integer
6 width = width_input.to_i # Convert width to integer
7 area = length * width  # Calculate rectangle area
8 puts area   # Display area
```

Step 4: Test the Code in the Computer

Similarly those who are adventurous can type the code lines from step 3 into a file and run the code from there. For those who are unsure, no worries; we address files later on. For now, simply see if you get the desired results; if not, make sure you typed everything correctly.

If it works, congratulations! You have just created a program that calculates the area of a rectangle.

3.6 Common Programming Errors

Syntax Errors

As a programmer, it is important for you to become comfortable with error messages. Even the most experienced computer programmers will have a typo or forget a quotation mark regularly. When you first start, error messages will seem incomprehensible. Later, they will help you fix the problem quickly.

Try the following command in `irb`:

```
irb(main):001:0> x = 1 + "hello"
TypeError: String can't be coerced into Fixnum
     from (irb):1:in '+'
     from (irb):1
```

Syntax errors refer to code that Ruby cannot actually execute. Since it does not make sense for Ruby to add an integer to a string, it stops execution and informs you of the location where it had to stop.

Gem of Wisdom

Truncation refers to limiting the number of significant digits by discarding extra digits. Unlike rounding, truncation simply throws the extra digits away.

Let's move on to a more realistic example. When entering strings, we are likely to forget quotes once in a while.

```
irb(main):002:0> x = hello
NameError: undefined local variable or method 'hello' for
main:Object
from (irb):2
```

Wait! Why does the Ruby interpreter not just tell us that we forgot quotes? Ruby must guess what we intended. All Ruby knows is that we tried assigning hello to x. Since any string not contained in quotes is the name of a variable or a command, Ruby tries to find the value stored in a variable named hello. Since Ruby cannot find any variable named hello, it prints an error. It is important to start viewing code in terms of how Ruby might interpret it, but this is a skill that will take time to develop. Meanwhile, realize that errors will happen, and expect to be learning from them.

Logic Errors

Errors that Ruby cannot catch are logic errors. They are problems with a program that cause it to return the wrong or undesired result. For example, if you are trying to find the area of a rectangle, but you multiplied the height by itself instead of by the width, that would be a logic error.

The Ruby interpreter, the program that executes the Ruby instructions input by the user, does not try to guess that we meant to use a different variable. Logic errors are often much harder to trace than syntax errors because of this. To avoid them, it is often useful to look at your program and "play computer." That is, pretend that you are the Ruby interpreter, and follow the steps that will be implemented as the program is executed. From this point on, we'll use the words *Ruby* and *Ruby interpreter* interchangeably.

A more common error involves integer division. Arithmetic expressions that operate on integers will always evaluate to integer form. This happens even with division, where the result would otherwise be a decimal. Ruby does this by truncating the arithmetic result (chopping off the decimal place and all the digits to the right of it). For example, 5 divided by 2 will evaluate to 2 instead of to 2.5.

```
irb(main):003:0> 5 / 2
=> 2
```

If you get a wrong value using this computation in a program, then your final result will likely be erroneous, too.

3.7 Mixing Data Types

Ruby will always try to remain in the same data type as its operands. For example, if the integers 2 and 3 are added in Ruby, the result will also be an integer.

```
irb(main):001:0> 2 + 3
=> 5
```

Likewise, when adding two floats, the result will also be a float.

```
irb(main):002:0> 2.0 + 3.0
=> 5.0
```

When Ruby encounters two operands of different data types, it will convert them to match where possible.

```
irb(main):003:0> 2 + 3.0
=> 5.0
```

The issue of dividing integers like 5 / 2 can finally be resolved. We are able to force Ruby to convert integer expressions into float expressions. Simply throw a float into the mix.

```
irb(main):004:0> 1.0 * 5 / 2
=> 2.5
```

Of course, it is sometimes impossible to convert the data types to match. In this case, Ruby will output a TypeError.

```
irb(main):005:0> x = 1 + "hello"
TypeError: String can't be coerced into Fixnum
    from (irb):4:in '+'
    from (irb):4
```

3.8 Summary

We discussed classes, variables, constants, and key data types such as strings and integers. At this point, you should know how to create a variable in Ruby and how to assign values to your newly created variable.

3.8.1 Key Concepts

- Ruby programs can be created/edited in any text editor (as defined previously), so long as the editor can save files as plain text. It is highly recommended that you use an editor suited for writing programs.

- When naming *variables*, it is a common practice to separate each word in a variable name with an underscore (_).

- Programming languages use various data types to perform various operations. Ruby uses many data types, including *integer* (*Fixnum* and *Bignum*), *float*, *string*, and *Boolean*.

- It is important to understand the syntax behind simple mathematical operators. Mathematical operators will often be used when programming. Pay attention to the order of operation.

- To output information onto the screen, use the `puts` command. To input information from the user, use the `gets` command.

- The three types of programming errors are *syntax errors*, *logic errors*, and *type errors*. Type errors often arise from mixing data types that cannot be mixed, such as integers and strings.

- *Conversion errors* are a subset of *type errors*.

3.8.2 Key Definitions

- *Variable*: A piece of data attached to a name, class, and memory location.

- *Instantiate*: In this simple initial presentation, creating a variable. See Chapter 9 for more information.

- *Constant*: A variable that is set once and never changed.

- *Initialize*: To assign a value to a variable when the variable is created.

- *Data class*: Information about the variable that defines the possible values a variable can have and what operations can be performed using it. A more complete description is presented in Chapter 8.

- *Integer*: A class that defines a whole number. Ruby recognizes two classes:
  — *Fixnum*: An integer with a limited range. In 32-bit systems, the range −2,147,483,648 to 2,147,483,647.
  — *Bignum*: An integer outside the range of Fixnum.

- *Float*: A class that defines a decimal number.

- *String*: A class that defines a sequence of characters.

- *Boolean*: A class that defines a value of either `true` or `false`.

- *Syntax errors*: Errors produced by incorrect syntax for the programming language.

- *Logic errors*: Errors produced by bad logic.

- *Type errors*: Errors produced by mixing data types that cannot be mixed.

3.9 Exercises

1. You saw that Ruby does not allow addition of floats and strings. For example:

   ```
   irb(main):005:0> 1.1 + "string"
   TypeError: String can't be coerced into Float
           from /Users/leland/.irbrc:73(irb):1:in '+'
           from (irb):14
   ```

   What type combinations does Ruby allow to be added?

2. Using irb, initialize three variables, x, y, and z, each to some number less than 10. Design an equation with these variables using at least one multiplication, one division, and one addition or subtraction element. Have the computer do it once without parentheses, and then add parentheses to the equation and try it again. Are the answers the same? If not, why not?

3. Earlier in the chapter, we saw the following:

   ```
   irb(main):001:0> 1.0 * 5 / 2
   => 2.5
   ```

   Now, try typing the following code into irb:

   ```
   irb(main):002:0> 5 / 2*1.0
   ```

   This should have produced a value of 2.0. Why does it produce the value 2.0, and not 2.5, like we saw earlier?

4. Write the expected value of x after both lines are executed.

   a.
   ```
   irb(main):001:0> x = 9
   irb(main):002:0> x = x/2
   ```

   b.
   ```
   irb(main):003:0> x = 9
   irb(main):004:0> x = x/2.0
   ```

5. What is the expected result of c for each code group?

   a.
   ```
   irb(main):001:0> a = Math.sqrt(9)
   irb(main):002:0> b = 2
   irb(main):003:0> c = a/b
   ```

   b.
   ```
   irb(main):001:0> a = 5
   irb(main):002:0> b = 2
   irb(main):003:0> c = a/b
   ```

6. Suppose a program finds the average temperature for a given year. A user of the program is prompted to enter the average temperature values for each season of the year: winter, spring, summer, and fall. The program stores these values as floats in variables temp_winter, temp_spring, temp_summer, and temp_fall, respectively.

The final result is stored in the variable `avg_temp`. The program calculates the average temperature with the following line:

```
avg_temp = temp_winter + temp_spring + temp_summer + temp_f/4
```

However, when the program runs, the value of `avg_temp` is always incorrect. Briefly describe what is wrong with this line and what changes you would make to correct this error.

7. What is the difference between logic and syntax errors? Give an example of each.

CHAPTER 4

Conditional Structures

In This Chapter

- Flow of execution
- If-Then-Else statements
- Elsif statements
- Case statements
- Debugging

4.1 Introduction

The preceding chapter introduced core programming elements, including variables of various data types and the process of input and output. Now it is time to use these concepts within a new context: conditional structures. This chapter explains the logic of conditional structures and presents the tools that allow them to work. These tools include the `if` statement, the `elsif` statement, and the `case` statement. We will also address debugging.

4.2 Flow of Execution

Logic Flow

Every algorithm has some type of *logic flow*. It is very easy to demonstrate logic flow using a *flowchart*. Let's revisit the algorithm for driving from Chapter 1 but this time illustrate it using the flowchart in Figure 4-1.

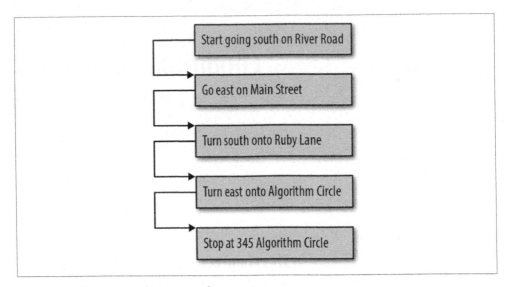

Figure 4-1. Flowchart directions of Figure 1-1

To properly move through the flowchart, start in the box that has the word *Start* in it, perform the step in that box, and then follow the arrow to the next box. Continue this process until there is nowhere else to go in the chart. If you walked through this flowchart, you would see that each step is performed once before moving on to the next step. This is known as *one-directional flow*. Algorithms with a one-directional logic flow do not really warrant a flowchart. However, not all algorithms are that simple, and not all flow is in one direction; that is, multiple possible execution flows exist. For example, Figure 4-2 shows a non-one-directional logical flow that models a choice between the two directions presented in Figures 1-1 and 1-2 found in Chapter 1.

To move through the flowchart in Figure 4-2, start in the uppermost box and follow the arrow to the next box. In this box, there is a condition and two arrows, but you pick one based on the outcome of the condition. After this, move on to the next box, and the rest of this diagram is one-directional. This type of flow, where a certain condition must be met to carry out the next step, is called *conditional flow*. We will talk about this in more detail later in the chapter. Also, later in the chapter, we refine the flowchart structure.

4.3 Conditional Control

When more than one flow option exists in the control flow, it is called a conditional control flow. Whenever a certain condition is met, its respective flow option is followed. A condition is an expression defined using relational and Boolean operators that

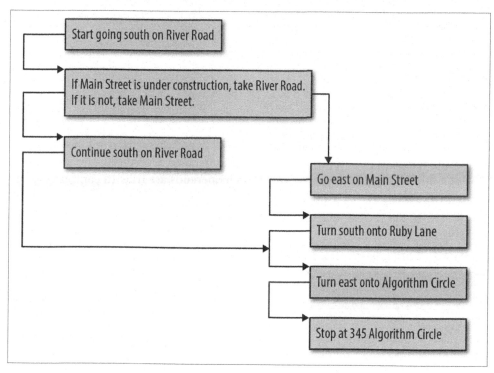

Figure 4-2. Multiple-path logic flowchart

evaluate to either true or false. The list and interpretation of the supported relation operators is presented in Table 4-1.

Table 4-1. Relational operators

Relational operator	Meaning
==	Equal to
!=	Not equal to
<	Less than
>	Greater than
<=	Less than or equal to
>=	Greater than or equal to

An example of the use of relational operators to form relational expressions is shown in Example 4-1.

Example 4-1. Relational expressions example

```
irb(main):001:0> 5 == 5
=> true
irb(main):002:0> 5 == 6
=> false
irb(main):003:0> 5 <= 5
=> true
irb(main):004:0> 5 != 5
=> false
```

To create complex expressions, simple relational expressions are combined by using Boolean operators. Two Boolean variable operators available in Ruby are and and or. The operator and evaluates to true only if both operands are true. In contrast, the operator or evaluates to true if either or both operands are true. To ensure the precedence you desire, a good programming practice is to use parentheses. A truth table is presented in Table 4-2.

Table 4-2. Truth table for and and or

A (alternate forms)	B	A and B A&&B	A or B A‖B
True	True	True	True
True	False	False	True
False	True	False	True
False	False	False	False

Recall the negation operator (!) that appears in the not equal to relational operator. This operator is a simple negation and works on any true or false expressions or conditionals, as shown in Example 4-2. Sometimes the negation operator ! is denoted by the word not. In fact, the fifth example in the figure, regardless of the Boolean values you set for first and second, will always evaluate to true. This is called a *tautology*.

Example 4-2. Boolean expressions example

```
irb(main):001:0> !false
=> true
irb(main):002:0> !(true or false)
=> false
irb(main):003:0> first=true
=> true
irb(main):004:0> second=false
=> false
irb(main):005:0> (first and second) or !(first and second)
=> true
```

Control Flow

Control flow is logic flow in the context of a program. Just as algorithms start somewhere and show an order of steps until the end of the algorithm, so does a program. Programs have a starting instruction, and then instructions are executed in a specific order, and eventually the program ends. We use a flowchart to illustrate control flow. Figure 4-3 revisits the names example to illustrate control flow with flowcharts. Note that the start and endpoints of the algorithms are indicated by circular shapes (circles or ovals depending simply on the length of text contained).

This type of flow is known as *one-directional control flow*. Programs are not limited to one-directional control flow. In this chapter, we discuss programming constructs that allow us to change program control flow. Understanding this control flow is essential to being able to create and test (debug) an implementation of an algorithm.

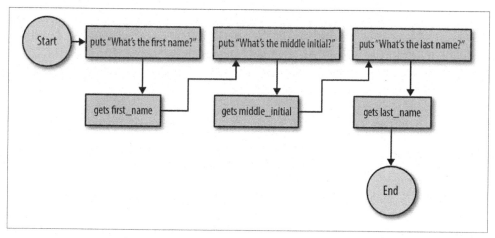

Figure 4-3. Control flowchart

Gem of Wisdom

An If-Then-Else statement or its equivalent is found in every programming language.

4.4 If-Then-Else Statements

Ruby uses an `if` statement for basic conditional control flow.

The basic form of an `if` statement is shown in Example 4-3.

Example 4-3. If statement

```
1 if (condition)
2   # section 1
3 end
```

The *condition* is a logical expression, as described previously; in Example 4-3, section 1 is executed when the condition evaluates to true, and it is skipped when the condition evaluates to false. An example of using the `if` statement is shown in Example 4-4. Given a number from the user, the program determines if the value is even. If it is, the program will print "Even" to the screen.

Example 4-4. Determine if the number is even

```
1 # if a number is even, print out "Even"
2 puts "Enter a number" # print message
3 number = gets.to_i # get number as an integer
4 if (number % 2 == 0) # check if even
5   puts "Even"
6 end
```

Assume the user inputs a value of 11. In this case, `number` will be equal to 11 when we try to evaluate the expression `number % 2 == 0`. This means that the flow option, shown on line 5, will not execute because the expression `11 % 2 == 0` will evaluate to false since 11 % 2 is equal to 1, not 0. Thus, nothing will be printed to the screen. If the user enters 10, then `10 % 2 == 0` will evaluate to true, meaning `puts ''Even''` will be executed; the screen will display "Even."

The `if` statement can be extended with the use of the `else`. The general form for the `if-else` statement can be seen in Example 4-5.

Example 4-5. If-else statement

```
1 if (condition)
2   # section 1
3 else
4   # section 2
5 end
```

Gem of Wisdom

Make sure you can step through Example 4-6 and understand each and every step. Play computer and consider different values for age; trace each step. What if age is 20? What if age is 5? Are there any cases where this program will not work?

This is similar to the first `if` statement presented; however, now there is a second flow option. In this case, if the original condition is not met, the second flow option is taken. For example, we can create a program that will tell us how much a movie ticket will cost based on a customer's age. Anybody under age 12 would get a discounted rate. We will call our program *theater.rb* and use the code shown in Example 4-6. Note that on line 13, we introduce the concatenation of two strings by using the + operator between them.

Example 4-6. Theater 1

```
 1 puts "Enter the customer's age: "
 2 # Get an integer age value from the user
 3 age = gets.to_i
 4
 5 # Determine the cost based on age
 6 if (age < 12)
 7   cost = 9
 8 else
 9   cost = 18
10 end
11
12 # Print out the final cost
13 puts "Ticket cost: " + cost.to_s
```

The logic flow of the code in Example 4-6 is shown in Figure 4-4. Note that another new construct in our flowchart uses diamonds. Diamonds represent conditional points. Each option of the condition is designated on an outgoing branch. The algorithm follows the branch corresponding to the value of the conditional.

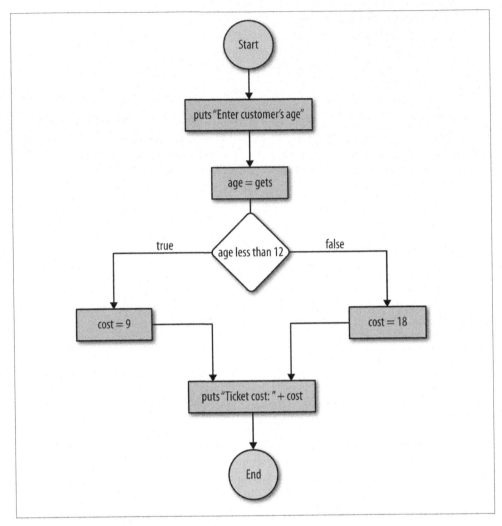

Figure 4-4. If-else statement flowchart

Testing Conditional Flow

Now that we have a program whose logic forks into separate paths, it is important to make sure that both forks work.

The movie theater will look unkindly on accidentally giving everybody a discount, especially if these moviegoers are not under age 12! We test the code stored in the file *theater.rb* by running at least one test in each flow option of logic:

```
$ ruby theater.rb
Enter customer's age:
8
Cost: 9
```

To test this for a higher value, we try again:

```
$ ruby theater.rb
Enter customer's age:
25
Cost: 18
```

Most errors occur on edge or boundary conditions. In our example, 12 is where the price switch happens. As such, it is important to test the value 12 itself.

```
$ ruby theater.rb
Enter customer's age:
12
Cost: 18
```

If this is not what you expected, then you are used to the way many companies work: if a person is age 12 or under, the person is considered a child. If the movie theater wants to abide by this standard, we will have to modify our conditional test to become less than or equal to.

Like most computer problems, there are many ways to achieve the same result. We could have changed the conditional to be "age < 13". However, since "age <= 12" better represents the real-world concept, it makes for code that is far more readable. The corresponding version of the program is presented in Example 4-7.

Example 4-7. Theater 2

```
 1 puts "Enter the customer's age: "
 2 # Get an integer age value from the user
 3 age = gets.to_i
 4
 5 # Determine the cost based on age
 6 if (age <= 12)
 7   cost = 9
 8 else
 9   cost = 18
10 end
11
12 # Print out the final cost
13 puts "Ticket cost: " + cost.to_s
```

Elsif Statements

Conditional flow can have more than two flow options by using elsif statements. The flowchart in Figure 4-5 shows multiple conditional flow and follows the code template shown in Example 4-8.

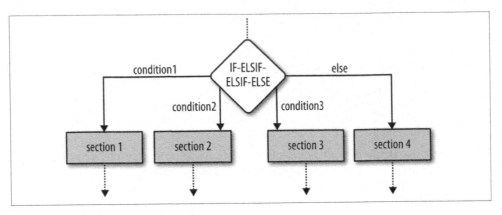

Figure 4-5. Elsif statement logic flow

Example 4-8. Elsif statements

```
1 if (condition1)
2  # section 1
3 elsif (condition2)
4  # section 2
5 elsif (condition3)
6  # section 3
7 else
8  # section 4
9 end
```

Only one of these four sections shown in Figure 4-5 will be executed. If none of the three conditions are met, the fourth section will run. Note that the first satisfied (`true`) condition encountered will be executed regardless of whether multiple conditions evaluate to true. With `elsif` statements, it is possible to expand to as many flow options as needed. Like the regular `if` statement, the final `else` is optional. If the movie theater decided to have different rates for children and senior citizens, the `elsif` statement would come in handy, as shown in Example 4-9.

Example 4-9. Theater 3

```
 1 puts "Enter the customer's age: "
 2 # Get an integer age value from the user
 3 age = gets.to_i
 4
 5 # Determine the cost based on age
 6 if (age <= 12)
 7   cost = 9
 8 elsif (age >= 65)
 9   cost = 12
10 else
11   cost = 18
12 end
13
14 # Print out the final cost
15 puts "Ticket cost: " + cost.to_s
```

The movie theater, however, may likewise decide to sell tickets at the children's discounted price for senior customers as well. We modify our example to include `age >= 65` in the discounted flow option, as in Example 4-10. Note that in this example, we use multiple conditions combined with a Boolean operation to form a single condition.

Example 4-10. Advanced conditionals

```
 1 puts "Enter the customer's age: "
 2 # Get an integer age value from the user
 3 age = gets.to_i
 4
 5 # Determine the cost based on age
 6 if ((age <= 12) or (age >= 65))
 7    cost = 9
 8 else
 9    cost = 18
10 end
11
12 # Print out the final cost
13 puts "Ticket cost: " + cost.to_s
```

4.5 Case Statements

Instead of using `if-elsif` statements, Ruby has another statement called `case` for handling multiple options. This statement is useful when presenting users with a large menu of different choices. The `case` statement is expressed in Example 4-11.

Example 4-11. Case statement

```
1 case
2 when (expression1)
3  # section 1
4 when (expression2)
5  # section 2
6 else
7  # section 3
8 end
```

After looking at a `case` statement in use, you may be wondering what would happen if multiple when clauses evaluate to true. Case statements are processed in order, so the first condition that evaluates to true has its corresponding flow option execute, skipping over all others. As noted earlier, this processing order is identical to the cascaded `if-else` statements.

We now update the movie theater example, where children, adults, and senior citizens have differing rates to make use of the `case` statement as shown in Example 4-12.

Example 4-12. Theater 4

```
1 puts "Enter the customer's age: "
2 # Get an integer age value from the user
3 age = gets.to_i
4
5 # Determine the cost based on age
6 case
7 when (age <= 12)
8   cost = 9
9 when (age >= 65)
10  cost = 12
11 else
12  cost = 18
13 end
14
15 # Print out the final cost
16 puts "Ticket cost: " + cost.to_s
```

4.6 Debugging

Basic debugging is a skill that every programmer must learn. When your program is malfunctioning and you do not have a clue where the error is located, you can use multiple puts statements to check the value of your variables at different times. Modify the code in Example 4-12 to use the assignment operator (=) instead of the comparison operator (<=) in the first conditional statement, as in Example 4-13.

Example 4-13. Debugging example 1

```
1 puts "Enter the customer's age: "
2 # Get an integer age value from the user
3 age = gets.to_i
4
5 # Determine the cost based on age
6 case
7 # '=' is assignment NOT equality test '=='
8 when (age = 12) then
9   cost = 9
10 when (age >= 65) then
11   cost = 12
12 else
13   cost = 18
14 end
15
16 # Print out the final cost
17 puts "Ticket cost: " + cost.to_s
```

If you run the example, it will not matter what age you input; it will always output the ticket cost as 9. This is because you are not comparing age to the integer 12 but instead assigning 12 to age, which is something that will evaluate to true. Edit the program to match Example 4-14.

Example 4-14. Debugging example 2

```
1 puts "Enter the customer's age: "
2 # Get an integer age value from the user
3 age = gets.to_i
4 # DEBUG
5 puts age
6
7 # Determine the cost based on age
8 case
9 # '=' is assignment NOT equality test '=='
10 when (age = 12) then
11   cost = 9
12 when (age >= 65) then
13   cost = 12
14 else
15   cost = 18
16 end
17 # DEBUG
18 puts age
19
20 # Print out the final cost
21 puts "Ticket cost: " + cost.to_s
```

By adding `puts` statements before the `case` statement and at the end of the program, you are checking what value is stored after it is entered and after the `case` statement was executed. If you run the new program, you will see that the first output will equal whatever age value you originally entered. However, at the end of the program, the `puts` will output the value 12, no matter what value was previously entered for age.

From this, you can infer that the value of `age` changed somewhere between the two `puts` statements. As you remember, we changed the comparison operator (<=) to the assignment operator (=). The assignment operator = is often mistyped when programmers meant to use the comparison operator ==.

Using `puts` statements to output key values is one of the simplest yet most effective ways to debug a program.

4.6.1 Alternative Styles of Debugging

Debugging your program includes printing intermediate steps. Further, it is highly advised—or more accurately, required—that you debug your program one portion at a time, rather than the entire program as a whole.

Another approach relies on one or more constants, possibly named `DEBUG_MODULE_1`, `DEBUG_MODULE_2`, and so on. In such an approach, these debugging flag constants are defined at the beginning of the program and set initially to `true`. In each corresponding section of the code, the programmer writes an `if` statement with the debugging constant as the flag that determines whether a `puts` statement is executed. Once the particular section of the program being tested is determined to be correct, the constant is set to `false`. This approach is shown in Example 4-15.

Example 4-15. Debugging example 3

```
 1 # Flag for debugging (change to false when finished debugging)
 2 DEBUG_MODULE_1 = true
 3
 4 puts "Enter the customer's age: "
 5 # Get an integer age value from the user
 6 age = gets.to_i
 7
 8 # Determine the cost based on age
 9 if DEBUG_MODULE_1
10   puts age
11 end
12 case
13 # '=' is assignment NOT equality test '=='
14 when (age = 12) then
15   cost = 9
16 when (age >= 65) then
17   cost = 12
18 else
19   cost = 18
20 end
21 if DEBUG_MODULE_1
22   puts age
23 end
24
25 # Print out the final cost
26 puts "Ticket cost: " + cost.to_s
```

Line 2 defines the constant to be used as our debug flag. Lines 9–11 and 21–23 represent code that should be run only during debug mode to help ensure that the program is running correctly. Compare the output of the code with DEBUG_MODULE_1 set to true and false.

4.7 Summary

We discussed how to implement conditional execution in Ruby. The if statement can cover simple conditions, and the case statement can cover more complex conditions. Relational operators, outlined in Table 4-1, were introduced, as well as their combinations and negations.

4.7.1 Key Concepts

- Every program follows a *control flow*, which is dictated by the *logic flow* of its algorithms. *Logic flow* and *control flow* can be better understood in a *flowchart*, and are often *one-directional* or *conditional*.
- Relational operators are the key to creating *conditional flow*. An expression that uses a relational operator is known as a *relational expression*.
- Another way to create *conditional flow* is through the use of advanced conditional structures. This is done by employing special statements, such as `if`, `elsif`, and `case`.

4.7.2 Key Definitions

- *Flowchart*: A tool for understanding the logic flow of an algorithm or the control flow of a program.
- *Logic flow*: The order in which an algorithm performs key steps:
  - *One-directional flow*: When the logic flow of an algorithm follows a one-directional order (i.e., a straight line)
  - *Conditional flow*: When the logic flow of an algorithm follows a conditional order (i.e., different conditions lead to different paths)
- *Relational expression*: An expression that uses a relational operator.

4.8 Exercises

1. Prompt the user for an integer and test if it's even or odd. Consider using the way Ruby rounds operations on integers when appropriate. Save this program in a file called *compare.rb*.

2. Modify *compare.rb* so that it:

   a. Prompts the user for an integer between 5 and 10 (inclusive) and displays whether or not the input was correct. Implement this using an `if`/`else` statement.

   b. Prompts the user for an integer between 5 and 10 and then informs the user if the integer was below the range, in the range, or above the range. Implement this using a `case` statement.

3. Write a program that, given two points on a two-dimensional graph, outputs a message (string) if the line that connects them is horizontal or vertical, or if the slope is positive or negative.

4. Write a program to solve a system of two linear equations. A linear equation is a mathematical equation that describes a line through its slope (m) and its y-intercept (b), and it will take the form $y = mx + b$. Make sure to account for the cases where there is no solution or where there are an infinite number of solutions.

5. The unit pulse function, $d[n]$, is very important in digital signal processing. This function is defined for integers only. It is equal to 1 when n is 0, and it is equal to 0 when n is any other integer. Write a program that prompts the user for an integer n, and returns the value $d[n]$.

6. Prompt the user for integers x, y, and z. Implement the decision tree shown in Figure 4-6 based on the values using if statements. Output how many of the variables are greater than 0. Note: each right flow option represents *false*, and each left flow option represents *true*.

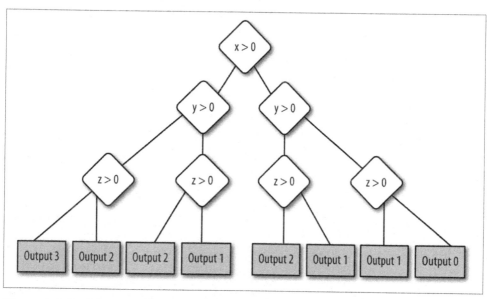

Figure 4-6. Decision tree for Exercise 6

Loop Structures

5.1 Introduction

The preceding chapter introduced conditional structures and the idea of logic and control flow. Now it is time to use these concepts within a new context: loop structures. This chapter explains the logic of loop structures and presents the tools that allow them to work. These tools include the *while* loop, the *until* loop, the *for* loop, and the concept of nested loops.

5.2 While Loops

The job of any loop is to perform iteration or repetition, and the simplest construct for doing this is known as a *while loop*. The general structure of a *while* loop is shown in Example 5-1. Its corresponding flowchart is shown in Figure 5-1.

Example 5-1. While loop construct

```
1 while (condition)
2  # statement 1
3  # statement 2
4  # ...
5  # statement n
6 end
```

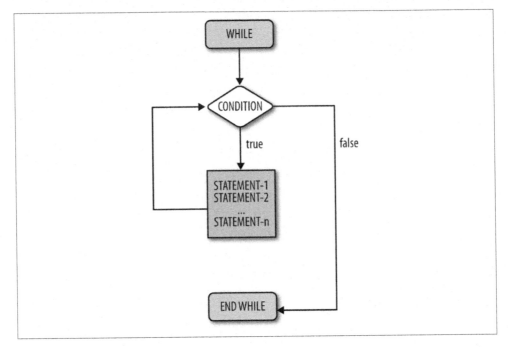

Figure 5-1. While loop flowchart

The control flow enters the while loop at the instruction: while (condition). This statement determines whether the control enters the body of the loop. If the condition evaluates to true, then the statements within the loop are executed. If the condition evaluates to false, then the control flow goes to the instruction, end, and the loop is exited. In the case where condition is true, the control flow will continue through all the statements between 1 and *n*, where *n* is any number greater than 0. Once a statement has finished executing, the control flow jumps back to the first instruction, while (condition), and the whole process starts over.

To clarify, a Ruby example is shown in Example 5-2. Its corresponding flowchart is shown in Figure 5-2.

Example 5-2. Counting program

```
1 n = 5
2 i = 0
3 while (i <= n)
4   puts i
5   i = i + 1
6 end
```

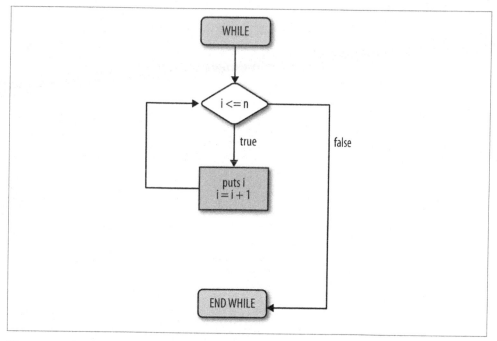

Figure 5-2. Counting program flowchart

The presented code is a simple program that prints every number between 0 and 5. Walk through lines 1 through 6 and make sure you understand the code before moving on. The loop repeats and prints the value in variable i and then increments the value by one. The loop continues as long as, or while, the value in i is less than or equal to the value in n. Every loop must eventually cause the condition to change; otherwise, it loops infinitely (known as an *infinite loop*). In the example, the variable i is incremented; so, after six iterations, i will be larger than n.

Gem of Wisdom

An infinite loop is a *logic* problem, not a *syntax* problem. Recall that syntax problems are things like misspelling `else` (try it sometime, and see what happens). Logic errors are much harder to fix, so take your time, trace the flow of execution, and step very slowly through the program.

5.3 Until Loops

The *until loop* is just the opposite of a while loop. Instead of occurring while some condition remains true, an until loop occurs until some condition becomes true. The code and semantics of the until loop are presented in Example 5-3. Its corresponding flowchart is shown in Figure 5-3.

Example 5-3. Until loop construct

```
1 until (condition)
2   # statement 1
3   # statement 2
4   # ...
5   # statement n
6 end
```

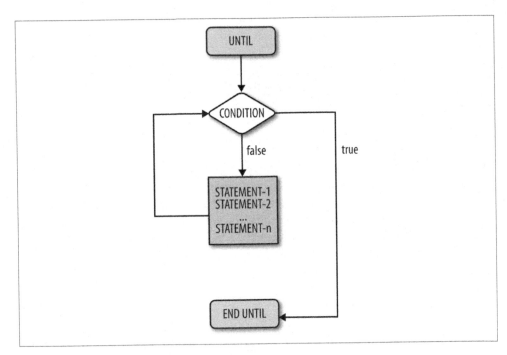

Figure 5-3. Until loop flowchart

Until loops execute the same way as while loops; the only difference is the way they terminate. If we want the counting program to work with until loops, only one line of the program needs to be changed: `while(i <= n)` becomes `until(i > n)`. The until and while loops are logical opposites, and the change in the counting program illustrates this, as a greater-than conditional operator (>) is used instead of less than or equal to (<=). Table 5-1 shows every logical operator and its opposite operator.

Table 5-1. Logical operators and their opposites

Operator	Opposite operator
==	!=
>	<=
<	>=

Switching from a while loop to an until loop is easy; simply switch the operator in the condition to its opposite. However, this raises an interesting point: these loop constructs are interchangeable. There is never any case where you must use an until loop instead of a while loop, or vice versa. A Ruby programmer could go her or his entire life only knowing one of these loops and never have any problem writing any program.

At this point you are probably wondering why both loop types even exist. The reason for having both is to improve the clarity of a program. Some things are simply expressed in a clearer manner with while loops than with until loops, and vice versa. Instead of saying "while this is not true" we can say "until this is true," and instead of saying "until this is not true" we can say "while this is true." Frequently it is easier for someone to understand a program that simply tests for the existence of true instead of not true.

In the counting program from Example 5-2, the variable i is a counter. Using counters is common to many tasks that require automation. Anytime a given set of instructions needs to be executed a certain number of times, we will be using counters. Ruby actually does not require us to set up the counter at all. Instead, it is possible to give a set of numbers for a loop to iterate through.

5.4 For Loops and Nested Loops

For Loops

A *for loop* takes a group of elements and runs the code within the loop for each element. This can be used to run a piece of code a certain number of times, or the operations can actually be based on the value. In Example 5-4, we see `puts  num` is executed once for each value of num. That is, the loop will execute six times, and six lines with numbers 0 through 5 written one number per line will be generated. The range of values for num is defined by the construct `0..5` (see line 1), which represents all the integer values between 0 and 5 inclusive.

Example 5-4. For loop

```
1 for num in (0..5)
2   puts num
3 end
```

Nested Loops

A *nested loop* is a loop inside another loop. Although all kinds of loops can be nested, the most common nested loop involves for loops. These loops are particularly useful when displaying multidimensional data.

When using these loops, the first iteration of the first loop will initialize, followed by the second loop. The second loop will completely finish before the first loop moves on to its next iteration. If that sounds confusing, the example in Example 5-5 should help you understand the concept. Its corresponding flowchart is shown in Figure 5-4.

Example 5-5. Nested loop construct

```
1 for i in (1..3)
2   puts "Outer loop: i = " + i.to_s
3 for k in (1..4)
4    puts "Inner loop: k = " + k.to_s
5 end
6 end
```

If you execute the program presented, you will see that the outer loop is displayed three times. However, between each outer loop, four iterations of the inner loop are run.

The flowchart illustrates the internal computation necessary to execute the code presented. The code itself, however, is easier to follow than the actual flowchart. Note thus the essence of using the proper code structure for a particular task.

Nested loops can be a powerful tool when displaying data involving both rows and columns. For example, it is possible to make a program that would print a calendar that displays 12 different months, and for each month, displays each day.

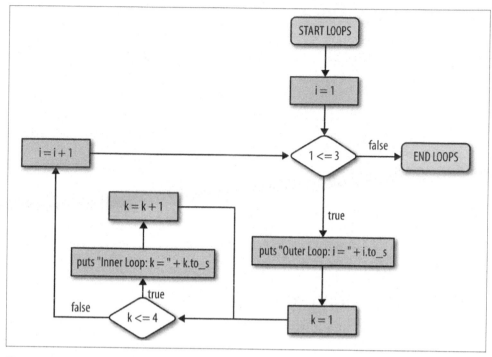

Figure 5-4. Nested loop flowchart

5.5 Infinite Loops

A classic problem, especially among new programmers, is that a small mistake can lead to implementing a program that simply will not stop.

Example 5-6 has an initial value of 5 stored in the variable i in line 3. The loop indicates that we should continue as long as i is greater than zero. Line 5 increments i. Hence, the loop condition of i > 0 is always true; so the loop will never terminate. When you run the program, it will look like nothing is happening, but in actuality, your computer is quite busy. It is happily repeating lines 4 and 5 forever. To terminate the program, hold down the Ctrl key and press C. This is an old key sequence that is an abbreviation for cancel, one of the arcane things you should memorize. (Ctrl-C cancels execution, and Ctrl-D ends the file.) There are a few other Ctrl sequences, but these two are all you need to make it through this book.

Example 5-6. Infinite loops

```
1 puts "Count from 0 to ? "
2 n = gets.to_i
3 i = 5
4 while (i > 0)
5   i = i + 2
6 end
```

Assume you realize that you are in an endless loop, and you want to fix it. Sometimes new programmers simply execute the program again *with no changes*. Let us assure you that if you do not make a change, nothing will change. The program will once again run indefinitely.

The secret to fixing an endless loop is to check the terminating condition and make sure that it will ultimately be satisfied. Hence, change something but do not change things randomly. Identify the cause of the problem, make a change that makes sense, and then test to see if your change has fixed the problem.

5.6 Example: Finding Prime Numbers

You now know enough to write numerous computer programs in Ruby, and we will soon finally be able to stop worrying about the details of a programming language and return to the fundamentals of computer science. In fact, at this point, you really know enough to compute mathematically just about anything that can be computed. To provide a little more practice with the topics we have discussed, let's return to our prime number example. First we present a Ruby implementation (Example 5-7), and then we explain the algorithm illustrated in detail.

Gem of Wisdom

Step through Example 5-7 and make sure you agree that this finds prime numbers. Does it think 7 is a prime number? Try 9. Try 17. Convince yourself that this approach works.

Example 5-7. Prime numbers

```
 1 # Initialize our counter
 2 i = 1
 3
 4 # i: [0, 100]
 5 while (i <= 100)
 6   # Initialize prime flag
 7   prime_flag = true
 8   j = 2
 9   # Test divisibility of i from [0, i/2]
10   while (j <= i / 2)
11     # puts " i ==> " + i.to_s + " j ==> " + j.to_s
12     if (i % j == 0)
13       prime_flag = false
14       # break
15     end
16     j = j + 1
17   end
18   # We found a prime!
19   if prime_flag
20     puts "Prime ==> " + i.to_s
21   end
22   # Increment the counter
23   i += 1
24 end
```

Recall that a number is considered prime if and only if its only divisors, commonly called factors, are 1 and itself. For example, 9 is not prime while 7 is. As hinted in Chapter 3, it is unnecessary to check for factors until you reach the actual number (minus one) since the largest divisor must be no greater than half the number itself. A prime number implementation can be optimized by using the knowledge that we can terminate the loop early.

The Ruby implementation shown in Example 5-7 includes a main loop that terminates at half the number rather than continuing until the actual number (minus one). Using this modification, we eliminate roughly half the number of loop iterations needed to determine if the number is a prime. If the number being tested is large, such a reduction can be significant in terms of the actual execution time.

Now let's go through the code in detail.

- Line 2 initializes i to 1 and defines i as an integer.
- Line 5 starts an outer loop to begin the prime number search.
- Line 7 sets a flag to true. The idea is that for each potential prime we assume it is indeed a prime number until we know differently.
- Line 10 begins an inner loop that tests all values from 2 to i/2.
- Line 11 is our first example of the debugging process we discussed at the end of Chapter 4. As seen in our prime number implementation, we commented out line 11. Thus, the computer simply skips everything from the pound sign (#) until the end of the line. However, if we were in the debugging stage of program development and wanted to see the values of i and j at a key point, this is a great place to look at them. You can uncomment this line just to watch how this program works. Many people will tell you, "Put in some output statements to see what is going on," but part of the art to this is finding out the best place to put them so that they give you the most information with the least number of output statements. Too many output statements may overwhelm the programmer and result in having her or him looking erroneously for the needle in the haystack.

  Many real-world programs are filled with statements, like the one on line 11, that are commented out once everything is working. Programmers like to leave them in so that they will be handy if anything goes wrong in the future. Furthermore, although commented lines are nonexecutable, in trying to delete them you might accidentally delete executable lines. Thus, since their presence can only potentially help in the future, and their deletion might accidentally cause the deletion of executable lines, we strongly suggest that you never delete a properly placed debugging statement.

- In line 12, the key test is performed to see if the value we are testing divides evenly by a value between 2 and its half. If no remainder exists, the number divides evenly by something other than 1 and itself, and thus is not a prime. We then turn the flag off.
- Line 14 has a new command called break. The break statement is an optimization that simply says that, once you know that a given condition is met, there is no need to further execute the loop. In our case, we can terminate the loop once we know that the value is not prime; there is no need to test for any additional potential factors. That is, once we find any factor other than 1 or itself, the candidate number is not a prime number, so we can end the testing of all values. In our case, this means the next statement executed will be line 16.

  Line 14 is currently commented out. You should try the program once keeping the line commented out as is and once with it included in the execution. You should see that including the break statement results in the program running faster; you

Gem of Wisdom

Note that in line 23 of Example 5-7, we introduce a new shorthand construct known as op=, where the op can be any legal operator between two variables. So, a op= b means a = a op b. In line 23, the variable i is incremented by one.

may need to try to find all primes from 1 to 10,000 (change line 2 from 100 to 10,000) to really see a difference.

- Line 16 increments j, and line 17 ends the inner prime search loop.

- Line 19 executes for each value being tested, and if prime_flag remains true despite running through the entire inner loop, then the prime value is output. The to_s method converts the integer i to a string to display it (output) with the puts (output string) command.

- Line 23 increments the value of i, and processing continues. The syntax used to increment i adds, subtracts, multiplies, or divides a variable by a value and immediately stores the result in the original variable. We can use the shorthand notation shown on line 23 of Example 5-7.

Here is the output of this program. We changed it so that it checks for primes only between 1 and 25.

```
$ ruby prime.rb
Prime ==$>$ 1
Prime ==$>$ 2
Prime ==$>$ 3
Prime ==$>$ 5
Prime ==$>$ 7
Prime ==$>$ 11
Prime ==$>$ 13
Prime ==$>$ 17
Prime ==$>$ 19
Prime ==$>$ 23
```

We suggest that you do not look at the program we have supplied for too long and just look at the algorithm. See if you can write your own program to find prime numbers. Then just use our program as a guide if you run into any problems.

5.7 Summary

You are now able to write numerous programs in Ruby. You also now have a better idea of what an algorithm is. What remains are topics that simplify the writing of complex algorithms and programs.

5.7.1 Key Concepts

- *Loop structures* force the computer to repeat a set of steps until a condition is met. This powerful tool greatly decreases the amount of code that must be written for a task to be repeated.
- While loops, until loops, and for loops can be used to create a *loop structure*.
- *Nested loops* are loops within loops.

5.7.2 Key Definitions

- *Loop structure*: A structure used to repeatedly execute a set of instructions.
- *Nested loop*: A loop contained within a loop.

5.8 Exercises

1. For each of the following subproblems, convert the given loop type (while, until) into its opposite.

   a. while (x == 5)

   b. until

      (x < 7)

   c. until

      ((x != 0) and (y > 2))

2. Walk through the program in Example 5-8 and explain what it does.

   Example 5-8. Code for Exercise 2

   ```
   1 puts "Enter a number >= 0: "
   2 n = gets.to_i
   3 a = 1
   4 while (n > 1)
   5   a = (n * (n - 1)) * a
   6   n = n - 2
   7 end
   8 puts a
   ```

3. Write a program to calculate compounded interest using a while loop. The user inputs the amount deposited, the interest rate (as a percentage) per period, and the number of periods the deposit accumulates interest. Compound interest means that every period, your new balance is calculated using the last period's balance times the interest rate.

4. Implement the mod operator without using the mod operator but using a loop. (Assume the numerator is always greater than the denominator and both are greater than 0.)

5. Make a simple calculator. It should read in two numbers, apply an operator (+, -, *, /), and display the result. It should continue to do this until a condition of your choosing stops it.

6. Write a program that outputs the first 20 numbers in the Fibonacci sequence. In the Fibonacci sequence, the current number is the sum of the previous two numbers. The first two numbers in the sequence are 1 and 1.

CHAPTER 6
Arrays

In This Chapter

- Arrays
- Hashes

6.1 Introduction

In previous chapters, we discussed various programming structures, namely, sequential, conditional, and loop, which can be employed in algorithms and programs. This chapter will increase the power of these structures by introducing a new data structure that can be employed with any of them, that is, the *array*. A data structure is any organized means of storage, an array being among the simplest of structures.

6.2 Array Types

6.2.1 One-Dimensional Arrays

An array is an ordered list of variables. To get the idea, imagine a row of compartments, each of the compartments can contain something or be empty, and they are numbered sequentially starting at 0, as you see on the left side of Figure 6-1.

Arrays start counting their *elements*, or individual variables, at index 0, as the *index* is the offset from the beginning of the *array*. Index 0 is the position of the first element in any array that contains at least one element. Likewise, the nth element can be found at index $n - 1$. Starting at 0 and ending at $n - 1$ may seem odd, but it is common among most programming languages.

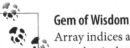

Gem of Wisdom

Array indices are the *offset* from the first element. As a result, the first element is stored at index 0.

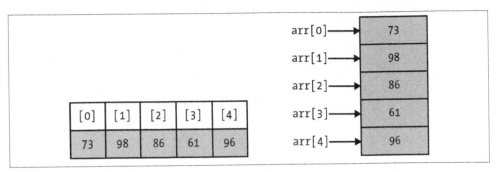

Figure 6-1. Diagram of an array and array access in Ruby

The arrays in Figure 6-1 are known as *one-dimensional arrays* because there is only one index or dimension. To access an element in an array in Ruby, the notation is `array_name[index]`, where `array_name` indicates the name of the array and `index` indicates the element of the array being referenced.

Consider an array named `arr` that stores a list of five test scores for a student. The student received the scores 73, 98, 86, 61, and 96. The first step of creating an array is the statement: `array_name = Array.new`. The example code in Example 6-1 shows how to initialize an array to store test scores.

Example 6-1. Initializing an array

```
1 arr = Array.new()
2 arr[0] = 73
3 arr[1] = 98
4 arr[2] = 86
5 arr[3] = 61
6 arr[4] = 96
```

The code shown is actual Ruby syntax for initializing array indices 0 through 4. The result of the code is much like the array in the righthand side of Figure 6-1, an array of size 5 with every element initialized. However, there is a quicker way to initialize an array, as shown in Example 6-2.

Example 6-2. Initializing an array

```
1 arr = [73, 98, 86, 61, 96]
```

Gem of Wisdom

Using arrays is a flexible and organized way of expressing multiple related items. Every programming language has them. As an abstraction, arrays are expanded variables. A variable holds one value; an array holds many. For example, to record names of multiple institutions using variables requires the use of variables such as `institution1`, `institution2`, `institution3`, and so on. With arrays, `institutions[]` stores all institutions.

No matter which way the array is initialized, the result is the same. To use the array, you access `array_name[index]`, as if it were a variable of the data type expected, as shown in Example 6-3.

Example 6-3. Changing the value of an element

```
1 arr = [5,6]
2 arr[0] = arr[0] + 10
3 puts arr[0]
```

The key advantage of arrays is highlighted when used in conjunction with loops. Since the syntax for accessing an element in an array is *array_name[index]*, we can use a variable for the index instead of literal numbers, as in the examples just shown. Thus, we can change the index in every loop iteration, and *traverse* or move through every element in the array. To know when to stop traversing the array, we can get the number of elements in an array by using the following statement:

```
arr.size
```

New programmers often make errors when dealing with the bounds of an array. These are the basic rules for array bounds:

- The first element in an array is at index 0.
- `arr.size` returns the number of elements in the array, not the highest indexed element.
- The last element in an array is at index `arr.size - 1`.

If we want to use a while loop to traverse an array, we need to initialize the index to 0 and increment it for every loop iteration. It is important to note that the condition in the while loop is `index < arr.size`, not `index <= arr.size`, for the reasons just mentioned. The code in Example 6-4 is an example of basic array traversal that prints out every element in the array.

Example 6-4. Displaying array content

```
1 arr = [73, 98, 86, 61, 96]
2 index = 0
3 while (index < arr.size)
4   puts arr[index]
5   index = index + 1
6 end
```

Running the code (stored in a file called *array_4.rb*) gives the following output:

```
$ ruby array_4.rb
73
98
86
61
96
```

However, in Ruby it is possible to accomplish the same goal in one line of code:

```
puts arr
```

This example is meant to be merely an introduction to simple array traversal. More practical reasons to use loops and arrays together are illustrated later.

Example: Find the Max

The example in Example 6-5 shows how to find the maximum of a list of five non-negative numbers. What would you need to change to support negative numbers?

Example 6-5. Find the max

```
 1 # Initialize array and loop values
 2 arr = [73, 98, 86, 61, 96]
 3 index = 0
 4 max = 0
 5
 6 # Loop over each element in arr
 7 while (index < arr.size)
 8   if (arr[index] > max)
 9     # Update max
10     max = arr[index]
11   end
12   index = index + 1
13 end
14
15 # Output calculated max
16 puts "Max ==> " + max.to_s
```

- Line 2 creates a new array named `arr` and initializes its variables.
- Line 3 sets a counter named `index` that will serve as an index into the array.
- Line 4 declares a variable called `max` that will be used to store the maximum number.
- Lines 7–13 implement a loop that scans every element of the array.
- Line 16 prints the maximum element at the end.

Each time the index variable `index` is incremented in line 12, the `if` statement in lines 8–11 tests to see whether the current value in the array indexed at `index` is higher than the current value in `max`. If the current value is higher, then the `max` variable is updated with the highest value.

Run this program, called *find_the_max.rb*. Your output should be:

```
$ ruby find_the_max.rb
Max ==> 98
```

As an exercise to make sure you understand the preceding code, change the example to output the lowest value in the array.

6.2.2 Multidimensional Arrays

Arrays that have more than one dimension are called *multidimensional arrays*. A common multidimensional array is the two-dimensional array, which can be used to represent matrices and coordinate systems. Unlike some other programming languages, Ruby does not provide built-in support for multidimensional arrays. The way to work around this is to put an array inside an array, which is essentially what a multidimensional array is anyway.

Consider the example in the previous section of an array that stores a list of five test scores for a student. Now, what if you had students with the following scores?

Geraldo: 73, 98, 86, 61, 96

Brittany: 60, 90, 96, 92, 77

Michael: 44, 50, 99, 65, 10

Table 6-1. Multidimensional array

	[0]	[1]	[2]	[3]	[4]
[0]	73	98	86	61	96
[1]	60	90	96	92	77
[2]	44	50	99	65	10

The best way to represent this data is to create one array with three indices and to have each index contain five elements. This is basically an array with three rows and five columns. To create such an array in Ruby, type in the following:

```
arr = [[73, 98, 86, 61, 96],
       [60, 90, 96, 92, 77],
       [44, 50, 99, 65, 10]]
```

By typing in this assignment statement, you have created a 3 × 5 table where the first, second, and third rows represent Geraldo's, Brittany's, and Michael's test scores, respectively. To access an individual score, use the format array[row][column]. So, if you wanted to know what Brittany scored on her third exam (remember, each index starts with 0, not 1), type:

```
puts "Brittany's Third Exam: " + arr[1][2].to_s
```

The output should be:

```
Brittany's Third Exam: 96
```

The rules for traversing a multidimensional array are similar to traversing a one-dimensional array, except you have to add a nested loop for each extra dimension. In Example 6-6, we illustrate how to print out each value in the array arr.

Example 6-6. Outputting multidimensional arrays

```
 1 # Initialize array and loop values
 2 arr = [[73, 98, 86, 61, 96],
 3        [60, 90, 96, 92, 77],
 4        [44, 50, 99, 65, 10]]
 5 row = 0
 6 column = 0
 7
 8 # Loop over each row
 9 while (row < arr.size)
10   puts "Row: " + row.to_s
11   # Loop over each column
12   while (column < arr[row].size)
13     # Print the item at position row x column
14     puts arr[row][column]
15     column = column + 1
16   end
17   # Reset column, advance row
18   column = 0
19   row = row + 1
20 end
```

Gem of Wisdom

Step through Example 6-6 and convince yourself that it generates the values you expect. What output values will be generated? What would happen if we added an `if` statement after line 13 that asked to skip values that were prime? Give that a try, as it uses our prime number work.

Like one-dimensional arrays, you can output everything using one line of code:

```
puts arr
```

The only problem with this statement is that Ruby will list all the values without any formatting. So it would be difficult to sort through all the data. We address means to format output in one particular case as part of our tic-tac-toe example in Chapter 12. We do not address formatting generally in this book.

Example: Find the Max—Modified

In the previous example, we created a program that finds the highest score in the array. Now we will create a program that stores the five scores for all three students. Using what you learned previously, modify the program to find out which student has the highest score. Print out the highest score.

When you are done with your program, compare your program to the code in Example 6-7.

Example 6-7. Find the max, modified

```
1 # initialize the array and index/score variables
2 arr = [[73, 98, 86, 61, 96],
3        [60, 90, 96, 92, 77],
4        [44, 50, 99, 65, 10]]
5
6 row = 0
7 column = 0
8 maxscore = 0
9 maxrow = 0
10
11 # for each row
12 while (row < arr.size)
13     # for each column
14     while (column < arr[row].size)
15         # update score variables
16         if (arr[row][column] > maxscore)
17             maxrow = row
18             maxscore = arr[row][column]
19         end
20         # increment column
21         column = column + 1
22     end
23     # reset column, increment row
24     column = 0
25     row = row + 1
26 end
27
28 # output name and high score information
29 if maxrow == 0
30     puts "Geraldo has the highest score."
31 elsif maxrow == 1
32     puts "Brittany has the highest score."
33 elsif maxrow == 2
34     puts "Michael has the highest score."
35 else
36     puts "Something didn't work correctly."
37 end
38 puts "The high score was: " + maxscore.to_s
```

- Lines 2–4 initialize a 3 × 5 array called arr.

- Lines 6–7 initialize the initial location of the row and column to start traversing the array.

- Lines 8–9 declare maxscore that will keep track of the highest score and maxrow that will keep track of who has the highest score.

- Lines 12–26 implement a loop that scans each element of the array.

- Lines 29–37 compare the value of maxrow and output the corresponding person's name as the individual with the highest score.
- Line 38 outputs the highest score.

Intuitively, like the previous example, there is a marker for the highest score. Whenever the program finds a score higher than the current value of maxscore, it updates maxrow to contain the value of the row in which the program found the high score (line 17) and maxscore to reflect the highest score (line 18). The program then uses if-else statements to find out who has the highest score (lines 29–37). Notice again how rows 0, 1, and 2 correspond with Geraldo, Brittany, and Michael, respectively. When you run the program, the output should read:

```
$ ruby find_the_max_modified.rb
Michael has the highest score.
The high score was: 99
```

6.3 Hashes

Unlike arrays, which strictly use integer indices, *hashes* can use any data type as their index. What Ruby calls a "hash" is really a clever way of using a string data type to map quickly to a specific element inside an array.

The string is referred to as a hash *key*. Some kind of function must exist to map a string to a number. For example, a simple hash function could add up the ASCII codes for each letter and implement a modulo for the number of keys we have. A hash collision occurs when our hash function returns the same number for two different keys, which can be handled with various collision resolution algorithms. A simple collision resolution algorithm simply places all keys that have a collision into a *bucket*, and the bucket is sequentially scanned for the specific key that is requested when a collision occurs. A detailed discussion of hashing is beyond the scope of this book, but we wanted to illustrate the differences between a *hash* table and an *array*.

In most cases, strings are used to associate keys to values. For example, instead of using a two-dimensional array, we can use a hash to store student test scores by name as seen in Example 6-8. As shown, similar to arrays, line 1 creates a new hash structure. Likewise, element assignment, lines 2–4, follow the same process done for arrays.

Example 6-8. Example hash usage

```
1 scores = Hash.new
2 scores["Geraldo"] = [98, 95, 93, 96]
3 scores["Brittany"] = [74, 90, 84, 92]
4 scores["Michael"] = [72, 87, 68, 54, 10]
```

Gem of Wisdom

Arrays are accessed with a numerical index, as in `array[5]`. Hashes are accessed with a string as the index, as in `scores["Brittany"]`.

Example: Hash

To access Brittany's score, we could simply call on `scores["Brittany"]`. Of course, the string `"Brittany"` can also be replaced by a variable that holds that string.

Example: Accessing a Hash

Example 6-9. Example hash accessor usage

```
1 scores = Hash.new
2 scores["Geraldo"] = [98, 95, 93, 96]
3 scores["Brittany"] = [74, 90, 84, 92]
4 scores["Michael"] = [72, 87, 68, 54, 10]
5 name = "Brittany"
6 puts name + " first score is: " + scores[name][0].to_s
```

In line 5 of Example 6-9, we assigned "Brittany" to the variable `name`; so, assuming that the code of Example 6-9 is stored in file *hash_2.rb*, executing the code should display Brittany's first score on the screen:

```
$ ruby hash_2.rb
Brittany first score is: 74
```

It is possible to get an array of all the keys by calling on `scores.keys`. We can then go through each key by using a for loop. We can now rewrite the maximum score example to work for any number of students, no matter what their names are or how many scores each student has.

Note that in our example, the number of individual scores varies among the students. That is, in Example 6-9, both "Geraldo" and "Brittany" have four scores each, while "Michael" has five. The ability to have varying numbers of entries provides great flexibility.

Example: Find the Max—Hash

Example 6-10. Find the max—hash

```
 1 scores = Hash.new
 2
 3 scores["Geraldo"] = [98, 95, 93, 96]
 4 scores["Brittany"] = [74, 90, 84, 92]
 5 scores["Michael"] = [72, 87, 68, 54, 10]
 6
 7 maxscore = 0
 8 for name in scores.keys
 9  column = 0
10  while (column < scores[name].size)
11
12   if (scores[name][column] > maxscore)
13     maxname = name
14     maxscore = scores[name][column]
15   end
16   column = column + 1
17  end
18 end
19
20 puts maxname + " has the highest score."
21 puts "The highest score is: " + maxscore.to_s
```

We see that running the code from Example 6-10, stored in file *find_max_hash.rb*, will output the following result:

```
$ ruby find_max_hash.rb
Geraldo has the highest score.
The highest score is: 98
```

Note that the entries in this hash differ from the entries used in the array example.

Hashes cannot replace arrays outright. Due to the nature of their keys, they do not actually have any sensible sequence for their elements. Hashes and arrays serve separate but similar roles. Hashes excel at lookup. A hash keyed on name with a phone number as a value is much easier to work with than a multidimensional array of names and phone numbers.

Arrays refer to a sequence of variables where each variable does not have a name; instead, it is referenced by an integer index. That is, arr[i] refers to the *i*th element in the sequence, remembering that indices start at 0. In contrast, a hash table uses a key-value pairing to identify the particular entry. In the earlier example, we wish to access test scores based on a person's name. That is, the hash table arr['Geraldo'] identifies Geraldo's test scores even though Geraldo is not an integer. Such referencing supports both efficient access and logical correlations.

6.4 Summary

We discussed one-dimensional arrays, arrays of arrays, and hashes. These are constructs that often take students time to learn, so we strongly suggest that you work through all the exercises in this chapter to ensure that you have a full understanding of these concepts.

6.4.1 Key Concepts

- *Arrays* are structures that use a table format to store variables. The data stored in an array is accessed using numbers as an index starting at 0. They can be used in any programming structure, but they are most commonly associated with the loop structure.

- One key concept when working with *arrays* is that they can have an infinite number of *dimensions*. This means that a memory location within an array can either store a single piece of data or store an entirely new array.

- *Hashes* are much like arrays, except that rather than using only an integer to look up a memory location, any variable can be used as a key.

6.4.2 Key Definitions

- *Array*: A consecutively numbered list of variables.
- *Element*: A variable contained within an array.
- *Multidimensional array*: An array whose elements are also arrays.
- *Index*: The number associated with a certain element within an array.
- *Traverse*: To move from one element to another within an array.
- *Hash*: A data structure that can map any data type (key) to a value.

6.5 Exercises

1. Using the array `arr` with value a[0] = 9, a[1] = 2, a[2] = 5, a[3] = 4, a[4] = 3, determine the output of the code in Example 6-11.

Example 6-11. Code for Exercise 1

```
1 i = 0
2
3 while (i < a.size)
4   puts a[i]
5   i = i + 1
6 end
```

2. The code in Example 6-12 looks for the first two elements that are out of order and swaps them; however, it is not producing the correct results. Fix the code so that it works correctly.

Example 6-12. Code for Exercise 2

```
1 arr = [5, 22, 29, 39, 19, 51, 78, 96, 84]
2 i = 0
3 while (i < arr.size - 1 and arr[i] < arr[i + 1])
4     i = i + 1
5 end
6 puts i
7
8 arr[i] = arr[i + 1]
9 arr[i + 1] = arr[i]
```

3. Write a program that splits an array into two arrays where any element in one array is smaller than any element in the other array. Solutions are not unique, but equally sized splits are desirable. The input can be any size array less than 100.

Example input: [6, 45, 23, 65, 17, 48, 97, 32, 18, 9, 88]

Example output: [6, 23, 17, 18 , 9] < [45, 65, 48, 97, 32, 88]

4. There are many ways to store image data. One way is to store pixel data in a two-dimensional array. The pixel data is itself a three-element array that describes the amount of red, green, and blue in the pixel. The amount of red, green, or blue is a number from 0 to 255. Here are a few example RGB values:

```
red = [255, 0, 0]
green = [0, 255, 0]
blue = [0, 0, 255]
black = [0, 0, 0]
white = [255, 255, 255]
yellow = [255, 255, 0]
```

Suppose you have a picture and need to count red pixels. For a pixel to be red, it must be within the following RGB constraints:

a. The R value must be greater than 100.

b. The G and B values must each be less than the R value divided by 4.

Write this program. Use this sample data to test your program:

```
sample =
[[[ 65, 67, 23], [234,176,  0], [143,  0,  0]],
 [[255, 30, 51], [156, 41, 38], [  3,243,176]],
 [[255,255,255], [  0,  0,  0], [133, 28, 13]],
 [[ 26, 43,255], [ 48,  2,  2], [ 57, 89,202]]]
```

This sample has three red pixels.

5. Function-plotting software must calculate a function at many points to plot it. Given the function:

$$f(x) = \frac{x^4 + 17 \times x^3 - 416 \times x^2 - 612 \times x + 2500}{500}$$

a. Write a program that calculates and stores 100,000 values for $f(x)$ between $x = -50$ and $x = 50$.

b. Extend the program so that it searches for values for x that are very close to, or are, zero. How many x values between -50 and 50 make $f(x)$ zero? What are they?

6. The three witches in *Hamlet* can brew any potion provided they have the right ingredients. Suppose that five ingredients are necessary in making a health potion: eye of newt (eon), toe of frog (tof), wool of bat (wob), adder's fork (af), and tooth of wolf (tow). Four reactions can occur between these ingredients:

- 4 eon + 2 wob = 3 af + 4 tow
- 3 tow + 1 tof = 2 eon
- 1 wob + 2 af = 1 tof
- 4 tof + 7 tow + 2 af = 1 health potion

Assuming you can control the order of reactions, write a program that can calculate the maximum number of health potions one can brew with a given amount of ingredients. Here is example output:

```
If I have 34 eon, 59 tof, 20 wob, 5 af, and 20 tow, I can make seven
health potions.
```

CHAPTER 7

Sorting and Searching

In This Chapter

- Popular sorting algorithms
- Analyzing the complexity of algorithms
- Search algorithms

7.1 Introduction

Entire books have been written on sorting and searching with computers. We introduce the topic here only to stress, once again, that writing programs is not the target of computer science; solving problems efficiently and effectively with the limited resources found in a computer is the real goal.

It turns out that computers spend a tremendous amount of time sorting. Just as we discussed different algorithms for computing prime numbers, we will now discuss three basic, comparison-based sorting algorithms. None of these are truly efficient. Efficient comparison-based sorting is beyond the scope of this introductory text. Additionally, we introduce a *radix sort*, one that capitalizes on the nature of the elements stored, rather than individual comparison between elements.

The sorting problem is described as follows:

Given a list of elements provided as input in any arbitrary order, these elements having an established ordinal value, namely a collating sequence, reorder them so that they appear according to their ordinal value from lowest to highest.

For example, consider the following list of numbers as input: 5, 3, 7, 5, 2, 9. A sorted output corresponding to this input is: 2, 3, 5, 5, 7, 9.

Gem of Wisdom

A common conjecture is that computers around the world spend the majority of their time sorting. Hence, it is difficult to talk much about computer science without talking about sorting. There are many sorting approaches.

In the following subsections, we will describe three comparison-based sorting algorithms and briefly compare them to demonstrate how to determine which one is the best. The implementation of each sorting algorithm will be presented in the context of grades for a final exam in a programming class. We want to provide a sorted list of the final scores, shown as percentages, to the students given an unsorted list. In each case, we describe the algorithm in plain language and then provide a corresponding Ruby implementation. Once the algorithms are presented, we discuss how we measure the notion of "best."

7.1.1 Selection Sort

Selection sort is the simplest to explain and the most intuitive. Imagine you have a deck of cards in your hand, and they have numbers on them. If you wanted to sort them, one easy way is to just select the smallest number in the deck and bring it to the top. Now repeat the process for all cards other than the one that you just did. If you repeated this process until the entire deck was selected, you would end up with a sorted deck of cards. The algorithm just described is *selection sort*.

The selection sort algorithm is formally defined as follows:

1. Start with the entire list marked as unprocessed.

2. Find the smallest element in the yet unprocessed list; swap it with the element that is in the first position of the unprocessed list; reset the unprocessed list starting with the second element.

3. Repeat step 2 for an additional $n - 2$ times for the remaining $n - 1$ numbers in the list. After $n - 1$ iterations, the nth element, by definition, is the largest and is in the correct location.

   We've already discussed arrays, so our Ruby code will first initialize an array and populate it with randomly generated numbers. The rand(x) function, where x is an integer, returns a randomly generated integer in the range [0, x].

The Ruby code for the selection sort is given in Example 7-1.

Example 7-1. Code for selection sort

```
1 # Code for selection sort
2 # 35 students in our class
3 NUM_STUDENTS = 35
4 # Max grade of 100%
5 MAX_GRADE = 100
6 num_compare = 0
7 arr = Array.new(NUM_STUDENTS)
8
9 # Randomly populate arr
10 for i in (0..NUM_STUDENTS - 1)
11    # Maximum possible grade is 100%, keep in mind that rand(5) returns
         possible values 0-4, so
         we must add 1 to MAX_GRADE
12   arr[i] = rand(MAX_GRADE + 1)
13 end
14
15 # Output current values of arr
16 puts "Input list:"
17 for i in (0..NUM_STUDENTS - 1)
18   puts "arr[" + i.to_s + "] ==> " + arr[i].to_s
19 end
20
21 # Now let's use a selection sort. We first find the lowest number in the
22 # array and then we move it to the beginning of the list
23 for i in (0..NUM_STUDENTS - 2)
24   min_pos = i
25   for j in (i + 1)..(NUM_STUDENTS - 1)
26     num_compare = num_compare + 1
27     if (arr[j] < arr[min_pos])
28       min_pos = j
29     end
30   end
31   # Knowing the min, swap with current first element (at position i)
32   temp = arr[i]
33   arr[i] = arr[min_pos]
34   arr[min_pos] = temp
35 end
36
37 # Now output the sorted array
38 puts "Sorted list:"
39 for i in (0..NUM_STUDENTS - 1)
40   puts "arr[" + i.to_s + "] ==> " + arr[i].to_s
41 end
42
43 puts "Number of Comparisons ==> " + num_compare.to_s
```

Gem of Wisdom

Selection sort works by repeatedly finding the lowest remaining number and bringing it to the top. Selection sort is explained first since intuitively it is the easiest to understand. If you are confused by Example 7-1, come back to it after a break. Please do not just skip past it and hope that the rest of the chapter gets easier. It does not.

- Lines 3 and 5 declare important constants that represent the problem. If the number of students in the class changes, we have to change only one constant.

- Line 7 initializes an array called arr that will hold the randomly generated numbers and ultimately the sorted list.

- Lines 10–13 step through the array arr and initialize each element to a randomly generated number in the range [0, *MAX_GRADE*].

- Lines 17–19 output the initial list so that you can examine its contents. Comment this out if you want to try a large set of numbers to sort.

- Line 23 is where the real work begins.

- Lines 23–35, the outer loop, ensure that we repeat the core of step 1 $n - 2$ times.

- Line 24 is the first line of finding the minimum value in the list. We set the first position of the unprocessed list to min_pos.

- Lines 25–30 iterate through the rest of the unprocessed list to find a value smaller than the item located at position min_pos. If we find such a value, as in line 27, we update the value of min_pos as in line 28. Once we have found the minimum value, we perform the latter part of step 2 and swap it with the first position in the unprocessed list. The outer loop repeats until the entire list is sorted.

- Line 26 counts the number of comparisons performed and is simply here for pedagogical purposes to determine the best sorting algorithm.

- Lines 38–43 output the sorted list and the number of comparisons.

Gem of Wisdom

Insertion sort works by leaving the first element alone and declaring it as a sorted list of size 1. The next element is inserted into the right position in our newly sorted list (either above or below the element we started with). We continue by taking each new element and inserting it in the right position in our list. By the end, all of our insertions result in a single sorted list.

7.1.2 Insertion Sort

Insertion sort is a little trickier than selection sort. Imagine once again that you have a deck of cards and that you are given an additional card to add to this deck. You could start at the top of your deck and look for the right place to insert your new card. If you started with only one card and gradually built the deck, you would always have a sorted deck.

The insertion sort algorithm is formally defined as follows:

Step 1: Consider only the first element, and thus, our list is sorted.
Step 2: Consider the next element; insert that element into the proper position in the already-sorted list.
Step 3: Repeat this process of adding one new number for all *n* numbers.

The Ruby code for an insertion sort is given in Example 7-2.

Example 7-2. Code for insertion sort

```
 1 # Code for insertion sort
 2 # Declare useful constants
 3 NUM_STUDENTS = 35
 4 MAX_GRADE = 100
 5 num_compare = 0
 6 arr = Array.new(NUM_STUDENTS)
 7
 8 # Randomly populate arr
 9
10 for i in (0..NUM_STUDENTS - 1)
11   arr[i] = rand(MAX_GRADE + 1)
12 end
13
14 # Output randomly generated array
15 puts "Input array:"
16 for i in (0..NUM_STUDENTS - 1)
17   puts "arr[" + i.to_s + "] ==> " + arr[i].to_s
18 end
19
20 # Now let's use an insertion sort
21 # Insert lowest number in the array at the right place in the array
22 for i in (0..NUM_STUDENTS - 1)
23   # Now start at current bottom and move toward arr[i]
24   j = i
25   done = false
26   while ((j > 0) and (! done))
27     num_compare = num_compare + 1
28     # If the bottom value is lower than values above it, swap it until it
29     # lands in a place where it is not lower than the next item above it
30     if (arr[j] < arr[j - 1])
31       temp = arr[j - 1]
32       arr[j - 1] = arr[j]
33       arr[j] = temp
34     else
35       done = true
36     end
37     j = j - 1
38   end
39 end
40
41 # Now output the sorted array
42 puts "Sorted array:"
43 for i in (0..NUM_STUDENTS - 1)
44   puts "arr[" + i.to_s + "] ==> " + arr[i].to_s
45 end
46 puts "Number of Comparisons ==> " + num_compare.to_s
```

Gem of Wisdom

Bubble sort is a little tricky. It is not how people would likely sort. The premise is that if we repeatedly place successive elements in order, eventually the smallest element will bubble up to the top. It is clever and sometimes is more efficient than the other algorithms we have discussed. So it is worth knowing. Take some time and step through this code.

- Lines 22–39 contain the core outer loop that inserts the next number in the list into the right place.
- Lines 26–38 contain the inner loop that swaps numbers starting at the beginning of the unsorted list until the number falls into the right place.
- Once the number is in the right place, the flag done is set to true in line 35.

7.1.3 Bubble Sort

Bubble sort is based on percolation; that is, elements successively percolate to the right order by swapping neighboring elements. This is like continuously and repetitively comparing adjacent pairs of cards within your deck.

The bubble sort uses two relatively straightforward loops. The outer loop ensures that the core process in the inner loop is repeated $n - 1$ times. The core process is to loop through the list and, for any successive elements in the list, check the following: if the value we are currently examining is larger than the next member of the list, simply swap those two values. Thus, each value will fall down the list into its proper place. Essentially, small values "bubble" to the top of the list, hence the name "bubble sort."

The bubble sort algorithm is formally defined as follows:

Step 1: Loop through all entries of the list.
Step 2: Compare each entry to all successive entries and swap entries if they are out of order.
Step 3: Repeat this process a total of $n - 1$ times.

The Ruby code is given in Example 7-3. An efficiency optimization (not shown) terminates the processing once no swaps occur. This conceptually does not affect the efficiency of the sort, but typically does so in practice.

Example 7-3. Code for bubble sort

```
1  # Code for bubble sort
2  NUM_STUDENTS = 35
3  # Max grade of 100%
4  MAX_GRADE = 100
5  num_compare = 0
6  arr = Array.new(NUM_STUDENTS)
7
8  # Randomly put some final exam grades into arr
9
10 for i in (0..NUM_STUDENTS - 1)
11   arr[i] = rand(MAX_GRADE + 1)
12 end
13
14 # Output randomly generated array
15 puts "Input array:"
16 for i in (0..NUM_STUDENTS - 1)
17   puts "arr[" + i.to_s + "] ==> " + arr[i].to_s
18 end
19
20 # Now let's use bubble sort. Swap pairs iteratively as we loop through the
21 # array from the beginning of the array to the second-to-last value
22 for i in (0..NUM_STUDENTS - 2)
23   # From arr[i + 1] to the end of the array
24   for j in ((i + 1)..NUM_STUDENTS - 1)
25     num_compare = num_compare + 1
26     # If the first value is greater than the second value, swap them
27     if (arr[i] > arr[j])
28       temp = arr[j]
29       arr[j] = arr[i]
30       arr[i] = temp
31     end
32   end
33 end
34
35 # Now output the sorted array
36 puts "Sorted array:"
37 for i in (0..NUM_STUDENTS - 1)
38   puts "arr[" + i.to_s + "] ==> " + arr[i].to_s
39 end
40 puts "Number of Comparisons ==> " + num_compare.to_s
```

- Lines 22–33 contain the core algorithm.

- Lines 24–32 contain the inner loop that swaps all elements that are larger than their next successive element.

7.1.4 Radix Sort

The *radix sort* is very different from the others. The sorting algorithms we have discussed compare the entire number with other numbers in the list and ultimately make a decision as to where an element belongs based on its number. The radix sort works by sorting the list by each successive digit. The idea is that if we first sort all the units or ones digits in a list and then sort all the tens digits and so on, ultimately, when we run out of digits, we will have a sorted list. Sorting by a single digit can be done by running one of the three sorting algorithms we have discussed. It can also be done by storing all values that match the digit in an array. We use this method so that the algorithm ends up looking very different from the algorithms we have already discussed.

Let's make sure we are clear about the idea of sorting values one digit at a time.

Consider a list of values:

    47
    21
    90

Now let's sort them based only on their rightmost digit. The rightmost digits are 7, 1, 0. We can sort these as 0, 1, 7. Now let's look at our list:

    90
    21
    47

It is clearly not in sorted order (but at least the rightmost digit is nicely sorted).

Now we move on to the next digit. It is 9, 2, 4. Sorting this, we obtain 2, 4, 9. Here is the list:

    21
    47
    90

Gem of Wisdom

In radix sort, unlike the other sorting algorithms discussed, no comparison of elements is made. Instead, radix sort repeatedly sorts elements digit by digit, commencing from the rightmost digit until the last digit is done. Radix sort illustrates that there are numerous unique approaches to the sorting problem; thus, investigate alternatives rather than simply selecting the first solution that comes to mind.

It is now sorted. You may wonder why we start at the rightmost digit. The reason is that we know every number has at least one digit, so we can start there. Some numbers may be bigger or smaller than others, so we have to start at the right and work our way to the left. Now let's consider the use of a hash. For the same example, we start with:

47
21
90

Now let's make a hash bucket for each possible digit, so we have a bucket for 0, a bucket for 1, and finally a bucket for 9.

We read the rightmost digit and put it into the correct bucket. This results in:

0 → 90
1 → 21
7 → 47

We now read the buckets in order from 0 to 9 and output all values in the bucket to continue the sort. This yields:

90
21
47

This is the same place we were at when we sorted the rightmost digit. This works because we process the hash buckets in order from 0 to 9. Now we repopulate our hash buckets with the tens digit. We obtain:

2 → 21
4 → 47
9 → 90

Reading the buckets in order gives us our sorted result of 21, 47, 90.

To review, we are building a hash of the following form:

0 → [Array of matching values for the digit 0]
1 → [Array of matching values for the digit 1]
...
9 → [Array of matching values for the digit 9]

It can be seen that our hash of 10 entries (one for each digit) points to an array of matches for that specific digit. Note that this works because we know we are sorting only one digit at a time, and we know the full set of valid digits.

The code for radix sort is shown in Example 7-4.

Example 7-4. Code for radix sort

```
 1 # Code for radix sort
 2 NUM_STUDENTS = 35
 3 MAX_GRADE = 100
 4 arr = Array.new(NUM_STUDENTS)
 5
 6 # Randomly put some grades into the array *as strings*
 7 for i in (0..NUM_STUDENTS - 1)
 8   arr[i] = rand(MAX_GRADE + 1).to_s
 9 end
10
11 # Output array and find the maximum number of digits in the generated array
12 puts "Input array: "
13 max_length = 0
14 for i in (0..NUM_STUDENTS - 1)
15   puts "arr[" + i.to_s + "] ==> " + arr[i]
16   if arr[i].length > max_length
17     max_length = arr[i].length
18   end
19 end
20 puts "Max length ==> " + max_length.to_s
21
22 # Add 0 padding based on the max length, simplifying the sort algorithm
23 for i in (0..NUM_STUDENTS - 1)
24   arr[i] = arr[i].rjust(max_length, "0")
25 end
26
27 # Now let's use a radix sort. Go through each digit and
28 # add each element to an array corresponding to the digits.
29 for i in (0..max_length - 1)
30   # Clear out and reset the bucket
31   buckets = Hash.new()
32   for j in 0..9
33     buckets[j.to_s] = Array.new()
34   end
35
36   # Add each number to its respective digit bucket
37   for j in 0..NUM_STUDENTS - 1
38     num = arr[j]
39     digit = num[max_length - 1 - i]
40     buckets[digit].push(num)
41   end
42   # Flatten the buckets into a one-dimensional array
43   arr = buckets.values.flatten
44 end
45
46 # Now output the sorted array
47 puts "Sorted array:"
48 for i in (0..NUM_STUDENTS - 1)
49   puts "arr[" + i.to_s + "] ==> " + arr[i].to_s
50 end
```

- Lines 2–9 initialize the list to be sorted as we have described in all the other sorts. Notice that we are storing the numbers as strings, rather than integers, so we can easily access the individual digits of the number. The list is initialized with random values.

- One addition is a loop, on lines 23–25, that right-justifies the array elements in the list using the Ruby `rjust` function. This pads the numbers in the list with leading zeros.

  Since we are going to loop through the entries in the list digit by digit, it is crucial that all numbers contain the same number of digits. Padding with zeros in the front of the number is the best way to ensure that all numbers are of the same length.

- Lines 29–44 contain the outer loop that processes the list one digit at a time. For each digit, the entire list will be traversed.

- On lines 31–34, we reset the hash named `bucket` that we discussed in the description of the algorithm.

- Lines 37–41 are the inner loop that adds each number to its corresponding bucket.

- Line 43 uses two functions, `values` and `flatten`, to give a new array representing the values sorted according to the current digit we are processing. The `values` function returns an array of all the values in a hash, which is analogous to the keys function discussed in Section 6.3, "Hashes." The `flatten` function takes a two-dimensional array and returns a one-dimensional array with the same elements, as shown in the following `irb` session:

```
irb(main):001:0> arr = [[1, 2], [3, 4], [5, 6]]
=> [[1, 2], [3, 4], [5, 6]]
irb(main):002:0> arr.flatten
=> [1, 2, 3, 4, 5, 6]
```

7.2 Complexity Analysis

To evaluate an algorithm, a common approach is to analyze its complexity. That is, we essentially count the number of steps involved in executing the algorithm.

An intuitive explanation of complexity analysis is the following. We caution you that our explanation is clearly an oversimplification, but it suffices for our purposes. Given a certain input size, assuming that to process a single element takes one unit of time, how many units of time are involved in processing n elements of input? This is essentially what complexity analysis attempts to answer. As can be seen, it is unnecessary to determine exactly the computer time involved in each step; instead, we simply determine the number of logical steps that occur in a given algorithm. In reality, we can have families of steps (say, one family is addition and subtraction, the other multiplication and division). We then count how many steps of each family are required.

A simple example will be to evaluate the complexity of computing a^2+ab+b^2 for a large number, say, n, of pairs of a and b. Computing directly, we should have $3n$ multiplications and $2n$ additions. However, we can compute the same expression using $(a + b)^2 - ab$, which can be done in $2n$ multiplications and $2n$ additions (note that we consider addition and subtraction to be in the same family of steps). Thus, the second expression is better than the original. For very large values of n, this may make a significant difference in computation time. This is a very simple example, but it provides a background for our discussions of the complexity of sorting algorithms.

In complexity analysis, we forgo constants; thus, the distinctions between n and $n - 1$ in terms of complexity are nonexistent. More so, we often assume that all computations are of the same family of operations. In terms of our complexity analysis, it does not matter whether the list shrinks or grows; for simplicity, assume it shrinks.

Now consider the three presented comparison-based sorting algorithms. For all, the outer loop has n steps, and for the inner loop the size of the list shrinks by one with each pass. So the first time it takes n steps, the next time $n - 1$, the next time $n - 2$, and so on. Thus, the number of steps is:

$$n + (n - 1) + (n - 2) + ... + 3 + 2 = 2 + 3 + ... + (n - 2) + (n - 1) + n$$

If you add 1 to the rewriting of the sum, it becomes a well-known arithmetic series, and its total is $\dfrac{n(n + 1)}{2}$. So the total number of steps for these sorts is $\dfrac{n(n + 1)}{2}$ - 1.

Clearly, for any $n > 0$, $\dfrac{n(n + 1)}{2}$ - 1 is less than n^2; however, the complexity is still considered roughly n^2. The official notation is $O(n^2)$ and is pronounced "on the order of" or "big oh." The reason the complexity is $O(n^2)$ is because complexity is only an approximation, and clearly the dominant portion of $\dfrac{n(n + 1)}{2}$ - 1 is n^2. For our purposes, if you grasp the concept of the dominant portion to determine complexity, you are ahead of the game.

For the complexity analogies, cn^2, where c is a constant, is considered $O(n^2)$ for any finite c. For actual computations, however, the value of c may be important. Again, refer to a book on complexity theory to understand, in detail, this important concept. For a reading list on algorithms and complexity, see Appendix A.

As an aside, order computation typically involves best-, average-, and worst-case analyses. For the selection and bubble sort algorithms presented, the best-, average-, and worst-case analyses are the same, since regardless of the initial ordering of the list, the processing is identical. As previously mentioned, there is an implementation of bubble sort that checks for no swapping with potential early termination. In such a case, the best-case analysis, which occurs when the initial list is already sorted, is $O(n)$.

Now let's turn to insertion sort, which is somewhat trickier to analyze. Here we are finding the rightmost element at which point to insert the value. For an already sorted list, the rightmost element will occur immediately, and we will end up at only n steps! Thus, the best-case analysis for insertion sort is $O(n)$. However, if the list is precisely the opposite of sorted, namely, in descending order, we must process until the end of the list for each step. Thus, once again, we end up with $\frac{n(n+1)}{2}$ - 1 steps. Thus, the worst-case analysis for insertion sort is $O(n^2)$. It turns out that the average-case analysis is likewise $O(n^2)$.

The radix sort works in $O(dn)$, where d is the number of digits that must be processed and n is the number of entries that are to be sorted. Hence, it should run much faster than the other examples. It should be noted that other algorithms—quicksort, mergesort, and heapsort—all run in $O(n\log(n))$ time. The radix sort might at first appear to be faster than these, but it depends on how many digits are processed. A 64-bit integer might require processing each bit as a digit. Hence, the runtime where $d = 64$ will be $O(64n)$. This might sound good, but $n \log(n)$ time will be faster where $n < 2^{64}$. So, in comparing the three sorts as presented, the average- and worst-case analyses for each on the comparison-based sorts is $O(n^2)$, while the radix sort can vary from linear time (sorting values with a single bit) to an infinite amount of time, as the number of digits is theoretically not constrained.

7.3 Searching

Searching a list of names or numbers is another very common computer science task. There are many search algorithms, but the key in developing a search algorithm is to determine which type of candidate search process matches the particular need. The following are the two questions (parameters) that affect our search algorithm selection:

- Is the list we are searching sorted or unsorted?
- Are the searched list elements unique, or are there duplicate values within the list?

For simplicity, we illustrate the search process using only a unique element list. That is, our implementation assumes that there are no duplicate values. We then discuss what needs to be modified in the algorithm and corresponding Ruby implementation to support duplicate values. Given the level of programming sophistication you now possess, we forgo presenting the only slightly modified implementation that supports duplicate values and leave it as an exercise for you. Once again, we revisit the final exam grade example we used in the sections on sorting.

We now discuss two types of searches. The first is for an unsorted list called a *linear search*, and the second is for an ordered or sorted list; it is called a *binary search*.

7.3.1 Linear Search

Consider the problem of finding a number or a name, or more accurately, its position, in an unsorted list of unique elements. The simplest means to accomplish this is to visit each element in the list and check whether the element in the list matches the sought-after value. This is called a *linear* or *sequential search* since, in the worst case, the entire list must be searched in a linear fashion (one item after another). This occurs when the sought-after value either is in the last position or is absent from the list. Obviously, the average case requires searching half the list since the sought-after value can be found equally likely anywhere in the list, and the best case occurs when the sought-after value is the first element in the list. The algorithm is as follows:

1. For every element in the list, check whether the element is equal to the value to be found.
2. If the element looked for is found, then the position where the element is found is returned. Otherwise, continue to the next element in the list.

Continue the search until either the element looked for is found or the end of the list is reached.

A Ruby implementation for unique element linear search is provided in Example 7-5.

Example 7-5. Code for linear search

```
 1 # Code for linear search
 2 NUM_STUDENTS = 35
 3 MAX_GRADE = 100
 4 arr = Array.new(NUM_STUDENTS)
 5 value_to_find = 8
 6 i = 1
 7 found = false
 8
 9 # Randomly put some student grades into arr
10 for i in (0..NUM_STUDENTS - 1)
11   arr[i] = rand(MAX_GRADE + 1)
12 end
13
14 puts "Input List:"
15 for i in (0..NUM_STUDENTS - 1)
16   puts "arr[" + i.to_s + "] ==> " + arr[i].to_s
17 end
18 i = 0
19 # Loop over the list until it ends or we have found our value
20 while ((i < NUM_STUDENTS) and (not found))
21   # We found it :)
22   if (arr[i] == value_to_find)
23     puts "Found " + value_to_find.to_s + " at position " + i.to_s + " of
       the list."
24     found = true
25   end
26   i = i + 1
27 end
28
29 # If we haven't found the value at this point, it doesn't exist in our list
30 if (not found)
31   puts "There is no " + value_to_find.to_s + " in the list."
32 end
```

Consider now the case of an unsorted list with potentially duplicate elements. In this case, it is necessary to check each and every element in the list, since an element matching the sought-after value does not imply completion of the search process. Thus, the only difference between this algorithm and the unique element linear search algorithm is that we continue through the entire list without terminating the loop if a matching element is found.

- In line 5, we initialize the sought-after value. Clearly the user would be prompted with some nice box to fill in, but we do not want to get distracted with user-interface issues. Ultimately the user fills in the nice box, pulls down a value list, or clicks on a radio button, and a variable such as `value_to_find` will be initialized.

- Next, a flag called `found` is set to `false` on line 7. This is used so that the search will terminate when the sought-after value is indeed found.

- In lines 10–12, the list is initialized and filled with some random values.

- The key loop starts at line 20, where the list is traversed one item at a time. Each time, the comparison in line 22 tests to determine if the element in the array matches the sought-after value the user is trying to find. If the value matches, a message is displayed, the flag is set to `true`, and the loop terminates.

- Finally, on line 30, a check is made to determine if the element was not found—in other words, is absent from the list. If this is the case, the value in the `found` flag will remain `false`. If it is still `false` after traversing the entire list, this means that no value in the list matched the sought-after value, and the user is notified.

7.3.2 Binary Search

Binary search operates on an ordered set of numbers. The idea is to search the list precisely how you might automatically perfectly search a phone book. A phone book is ordered from *A* to *Z*. Ideally, you initially search the halfway point in the phone book. For example, if the phone book had 99 names, ideally you would initially look at name number 50. Let's say it starts with an *M*, since *M* is the 13th letter in the alphabet. If the name we are looking for starts with anything from *A* to *M*, for example, "Fred," we find the halfway point between those beginning with *A* and those beginning with *M*. If, on the other hand, we are searching for a name farther down the alphabet than those names that start with *M*, for example, "Sam," we find the halfway point between those beginning with *M* and those beginning with *Z*. Each time, we find the precise middle element of those elements left to be searched and repeat the process. We terminate the process once the sought-after value is found or when the remaining list of elements to search consists of only one value.

By following this process, each time we compare, we reduce half of the search space. This halving process results in a tremendous savings in terms of the number of comparisons made. A linear search must compare each element in the list; a binary search reduces the search space in half each time. Thus, $2^x = n$ is the equation needed to determine how many comparisons (x) are needed to find a sought-after value in an n element list. Solving for x, we obtain $x = \log_2(n)$.

Gem of Wisdom

Binary search is one of the finest examples of computer science helping to make software work smart instead of just working hard. A linear search of 1 million elements takes on average half a million comparisons. A binary search takes 20. That is an average savings of 499,980 comparisons! So think before you code.

Instead of an $O(n)$ algorithm needed to find an element using a linear search, we now have an $O(\log_2(n))$ search algorithm. Now, for example, consider a sorted list with 1,048,576 elements. For a linear search, on average, we would need to compare 524,288 elements against the sought-after value, but we may need to perform a total of 1,048,576 comparisons.

In contrast, in a binary search we are guaranteed to search using only $\log_2(1,048,576)$ = 20 comparisons. Instead of 524,288 comparisons in the average case, the binary search algorithm requires only 20. That is, the number of comparisons required by the binary search algorithm is less than 0.004% of the expected number of comparisons needed by the linear search algorithm. As an aside, $O(\log_2(n))$ and $O(\log(n))$ are equivalent, since they differ strictly by a constant. Hence, generally speaking, the $O(\log(n))$ notation is preferred. Of course, binary search is possible only if the original list is sorted. The binary search explanation given earlier is for a unique element list only. However, before presenting the modification needed for potential duplicate elements, a few remarks regarding the use of binary search must be made:

- First, binary search assumes an ordered list. If the list is unordered, it must be sorted prior to the search, or a binary search won't work. Sorting involves a greater time complexity than searching. Thus, if the search will occur rarely, it might not be wise to sort the list. On the other hand, searches often occur frequently and the updating of the list occurs infrequently. Thus, in such cases, always sort (order) the list and then use binary search.

- The average- and worst-case search times for binary search are $O(\log(n))$, while the average- and worst-case search times for linear search are $O(n)$. What is interesting, however, is that unlike for linear search, where, in practice, the worst-case search time is double that of the average case, for binary search both times are roughly identical in practice.

In Example 7-6, we present a Ruby implementation of unique element binary search. Note that we introduce on line 16 a built-in Ruby feature to check if a value is already present within an array and on line 22 to sort an array in place.

Example 7-6. Code for binary search

```
 1 # Code for binary search
 2 NUM_STUDENTS = 30
 3 MAX_GRADE = 100
 4 arr = Array.new(NUM_STUDENTS)
 5 # The value we are looking for
 6 value_to_find = 7
 7 low = 0
 8 high = NUM_STUDENTS - 1
 9 middle = (low + high) / 2
10 found = false
11
12 # Randomly put some exam grades into the array
13 for i in (0..NUM_STUDENTS - 1)
14   new_value = rand(MAX_GRADE + 1)
15   # make sure the new value is unique
16   while (arr.include?(new_value))
17     new_value = rand(MAX_GRADE + 1)
18   end
19   arr[i] = new_value
20 end
21 # Sort the array (with Ruby's built-in sort)
22 arr.sort!
23
24 print "Input List: "
25 for i in (0..NUM_STUDENTS - 1)
26   puts "arr[" + i.to_s + "] ==> " + arr[i].to_s
27 end
28
29 while ((low <= high) and (not found))
30   middle = (low + high) / 2
31   # We found it :)
32   if arr[middle] == value_to_find
33     puts "Found grade " + value_to_find.to_s + "% at position " + middle.to_s
34     found = true
35   end
36
37   # If the value should be lower than middle, search the lower half,
38   # otherwise, search the upper half
39   if (arr[middle] < value_to_find)
40     low = middle + 1
41   else
42     high = middle - 1
43   end
44 end
45
46 if (not found)
47   puts "There is no grade of " + value_to_find.to_s + "% in the list."
48 end
```

We use these features to simplify the code illustrated. Note that this type of abstraction, namely, the use of the *built-in encapsulated* feature, simplifies software development, increases readability, and simplifies software maintenance. Its use is paramount in practice. It should be understood that this book uses Ruby as a tool for learning concepts of computer science and basic programming, and not as an attempt to teach all the capabilities of the Ruby interpreter. See the additional reading list in Appendix A if you are interested in exploring additional built-in features of Ruby.

- Line 9 computes the first middle range.
- Lines 29–44 implement the key loop that keeps cutting the search space down by half.
- Line 32 is the comparison to the sought-after value. If we find the element, we are done and we update the same found flag that was used for the linear search. If the value is less than the middle we update the high side of the range, and if it is greater we update the low side of the range. At the end, we verify that the sought-after value was indeed found.

As with the linear search algorithm, the modification required to support possible duplicate values is relatively minimal for the binary search algorithm. Since binary search requires an ordered list, if a sought-after value is found, then all duplicates must be adjacent to the position just found.

Thus, to find all duplicates, positions immediately preceding and following the current position are checked for as long as the sought-after value is found. That is, in succession, adjacent positions earlier and earlier in the list are checked while the stored element value equals that which is sought after, and similarly for later and later positions. Again, the implementation of this change is left as an exercise to the reader.

7.4 Summary

We discussed the various sorting schemes, both comparison-based and non-comparison-based, and the strengths of each. We introduced the field of complexity analysis, a tool used to quantify the performance of an algorithm. Finally, we discussed searching and provided a real-world example of searching techniques.

Specifically, we described four elementary sorting algorithms. The first three presented —selection, insertion, and bubble sort—are comparison based. That is, elements are compared against one another to determine a sorted ordering. The fourth algorithm, radix sort, differs substantially. Instead of comparing elements, radix sort orders the elements according to their representation, starting from the rightmost digit. Once all digits of the element representation are processed, the list is sorted. The complexity of these sorting algorithms is presented in Table 7-1, where n represents the number of elements in the list and k represents the number of digits needed to represent the largest element. The best-case scenario occurs when the original list is already sorted; the worst-case scenario occurs when the original list is in reserve order; and the average-case scenario represents an original random ordering.

Table 7-1. Sort algorithm complexity summary

	Best case	Worst case	Average case
Selection sort	$O(n^2)$	$O(n^2)$	$O(n^2)$
Insertion sort	$O(n)$	$O(n^2)$	$O(n^2)$
Bubble sort	$O(n)$	$O(n^2)$	$O(n^2)$
Radix sort	$O(kn)$	$O(kn)$	$O(kn)$

Likewise, we presented two searching algorithms: linear and binary search. Linear search can be used to search any list, whereas binary search requires a sorted list. The complexity of these searching algorithms is presented in Table 7-2, where n represents the number of elements in the list searched. The best-case scenario occurs when the first element encountered is the element sought; the worst-case scenario occurs when the sought after element is missing; and the average-case scenario represents a random list.

Table 7-2. Search algorithm complexity summary

	Best case	Worst case	Average case
Linear search	$O(1)$	$O(n)$	$O(n)$
Binary search	$O(1)$	$O(\log(n))$	$O(\log(n))$

7.4.1 Key Concepts

- *Sorting* is a common problem that occurs in many places in computer science. We focus primarily on *comparison-based* sorting, where we simply compare the items to determine the order. *Radix sort* sorts numbers without directly comparing them.

- *Searching* can be done naively by *linearly searching* through a list, but if the list is sorted, we can take advantage of *binary search* to improve performance.

- When discussing algorithm performance, computer scientists use *complexity analysis*.

7.4.2 Key Definitions

- *Comparison-based sort*: A sorting method that relies on directly comparing the elements.

- *Complexity analysis*: A mathematical way of analyzing an algorithm's performance.

7.5 Exercises

1. Radix sort, as presented, works for integers. Modify the algorithm in Example 7-4 to sort English names.

2. For each input sequence provided in the following list, state which presented comparison-based sort or sorts would require the fewest steps. Explain why.

   a. 5 2 4 3 1

   b. 1 2 3 4 5

   c. 5 4 3 2 1

3. You are provided a lengthy unsorted list and told to search it.

   a. Which search algorithm would you use?

   b. If you were told that you will need to search the list many times, would your search strategy change? If so, how?

   c. At which point would you change your approach if you were to change it?

4. The complexity of the comparison-based sorting algorithms presented, on the average case, is $O(n^2)$. Design a comparison-based sorting algorithm with a lower complexity. What is the underlying premise that lowers its complexity?

5. Generate a 100-element list containing integers in the range 0–10. Sort the list with selection sort and with radix sort.

   a. Which is faster? Why?

   b. Try this again, but with 10,000 elements. Note the relative difference. Why does it exist?

CHAPTER 8

Using Objects

In This Chapter

- Objects
- Built-in objects

8.1 Introduction

In Chapter 6, we discussed the concept of arrays and hashes, additional structures that can be used to store data. In this and the following two chapters, we discuss objects.

8.2 Objects and Built-in Objects

So far, we have been writing code that is procedural in nature; that is, code whose logical flow starts at the top and works its way to the bottom. Any computer program can be written in a procedural manner. However, when code gets long, it becomes difficult to debug and maintain. It also becomes redundant and dangerous to write the same code over and over. The object-oriented approach was created for dealing with these very issues. To switch to objects, you must understand why they are useful in the first place.

Imagine a product as complex as Microsoft Word. To produce it, a team of Microsoft programmers had to write millions of lines of code, with hundreds of people working on the code at the same time. To support simultaneous development, the code was segmented by functionality. Understanding how such complex products get subdivided into manageable pieces requires that we first understand the building blocks of such code. These building blocks in Ruby are *classes* that define *objects*.

Gem of Wisdom

Ruby is a truly object-oriented language, and that is one reason we picked it for this book. Objects usually correspond to entities that exist in the real world. They encapsulate values and support actions as well. While a variable might have a value 5, an object named `airplane` might have one value of `Boeing 747` and another value of `current location`. Also, `airplane` can have an action that says `fly()` that might change its current location based on how far it has flown.

8.2.1 Objects

Objects and object-oriented programming simplify the implementation of large programs. If you work on a program by yourself, it is up to you to organize your work. If you work with 100 other programmers, then everything must be nicely compartmentalized; otherwise, each programmer will constantly step on the other programmers' toes. There is nothing worse than getting your piece of a program to work and finding out that you inadvertently broke someone else's.

If you and your friend decide to work on a project together, you can easily run into trouble. Imagine if your friend makes a variable called x and manipulates it. You remain unaware of this changing of value. So later on in the code, you likewise decide to use a variable called x. Your piece of code and your friend's piece of code both work on their own, but when you integrate them, strange problems occur.

Objects are designed to separate key activities in a program so that once you get something to work, you need not constantly worry about accidentally breaking it when you make new objects. The activities are essentially isolated from one another. They can communicate information without the need to know how it is produced and what the specifics of the implementation are. For example, a programmer might build an object called `TicTacToe` when making a tic-tac-toe board game. Once the part of the program that draws the board works, everyone can just communicate with that object in a way that ensures that no one steps on another programmer's toes.

Objects enable programs to be compartmentalized so that programmers can work at the same time without fear of running over one another. Consider a construction crew building a house. Someone painting one room does not constantly check on the work of someone who is painting another room. This is because the rooms are compartmentalized—they have walls and ceilings that keep paint from dripping from one room to the other. However, two painters working in the same room must always be in constant communication to be effective and efficient. For example, if they were not communicating, it would be possible that one painter could drip paint on the other or paint the worker into a corner.

Objects are isolated pieces of code that have their own private chunks of data and private actions that can be performed with that data. The actions that an object may perform are referred to as *methods*. Object-oriented programming tries to create the most logical separation between pieces of code.

8.2.2 Built-in Objects

Without realizing it, you have been using objects since the moment you began to program anything in Ruby. In Chapter 3, you began using objects when you started using variables; you just did not have to think about it. In fact, everything in Ruby is an object, and this section will discuss some of the more common objects you will use.

An *application programming interface*, or *API*, is an interface provided to the programmer to allow the use of certain functionality without knowing the specifics of the implementation. When you downloaded the Ruby interpreter to your hard drive, you probably downloaded a copy of Ruby's API documentation with it, but in case you did not, it is available online (*http://www.ruby-doc.org/core/*). If you visit this site, you will notice it has three headings: *files*, *classes*, and *methods*. For now, we will focus on classes.

A *class* defines the characteristics and behaviors of an object. It contains the variables and the code necessary to implement the operations of the object, usually called *methods*. If you look through the list of classes, you will see there are many. However, you have already used a few of them. Some classes you may have already used are the array, Fixnum, float, and string classes. While there are many more classes than these, it is not required that you know what they do or what they consist of. However, it is required that you know how to use them when the time comes.

For any class, all the supported methods for the class are provided.

For example, the string class (see Figures 8-1 and 8-2) has a length method, `str.length => integer`. This means that if we call the string's length method, it will return an integer. The next part is simply a description of the method, and it does what one would expect a length method to do. The following is an example of using this method:

```
irb(main):001:0> "hello".length
=> 5
```

Simply put, we call the string class method length on the string object "hello," and we get back the number of characters in "hello," which is 5. This is a simple example of calling, or using, a method. However, calling a method is not always this simple. Let's look at another example of a method from the string class.

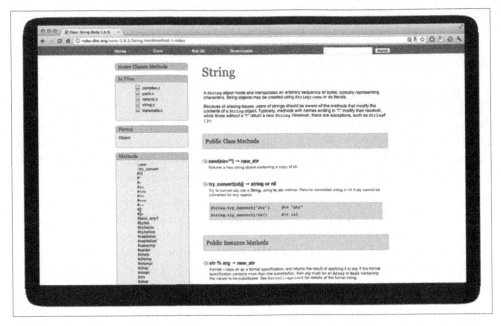

Figure 8-1. String API documentation

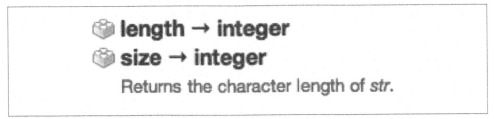

Figure 8-2. String's method: length

The example method in Figure 8-3 is significantly more difficult. It shows multiple ways to call the method index, along with the results returned when the method is called. By looking at the description of the method taken from the actual Ruby documentation website and written on top of the example calls, you may be able to decipher how calling this method works, but it uses concepts we have not yet discussed. The main concept here is that this method needs some type of outside data to work; supplying this outside data to a method while calling it is known as *parameter passing*.

Returns the index of the first occurrence of the given *substring* or pattern *(regexp)* in *str*. Returns `nil` if not found. If the second parameter is present, it specifies the position in the string to begin the search.

```
"hello".index('e')              #=> 1
"hello".index('lo')             #=> 3
"hello".index('a')              #=> nil
"hello".index(?e)               #=> 1
"hello".index(/[aeiou]/, -3)    #=> 4
```

Figure 8-3. String's method: index

8.2.3 Parameter Passing

Looking at the list of built-in methods, you will see that the syntax for some of them requires a variable in parentheses; these variables are called *parameters*. When using built-in methods with parameters, you are sending the value of the variable to the method to be manipulated. Consider the imaginary method called `multiplier` in Example 8-1.

Example 8-1. Parameter passing

```
1 x = 3
2 y = x.multiplier(4)
3 puts "The number is: " + y.to_s
```

Line 1 defines the variable x to be 3. The next line assigns a value to y by calling our imaginary method `multiplier` and passing the value of 4 as a parameter. If we looked at the output of this method, it would show:

```
The number is: 12
```

By looking at this, you can assume that the method multiplies the value of the parameter by a certain value. If we want to find out what the `multiplier` method really does, we can change the value of the parameter to 5. After doing this, the observed output is:

```
The number is: 15
```

You can now conclude that the `multiplier` method multiplies the value of the parameter by the value of x. The key concept of parameters in methods is that it does not matter what value is being passed; an output is generated using the same operations within the method every time. Think of the method as a black box, as depicted in Figure 8-4.

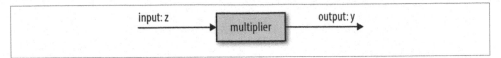

Figure 8-4. Black box for multiplier method

The system has an input z, an output y, and a black box. The input z is sent to the black box, which manipulates the variable and then outputs it as y. We do not know, nor do we care, what happens inside the black box. The only thing that matters is the resultant output.

Now let's look at an example using the actual Ruby built-in method called split. This method is used with strings and splits the strings into array elements based on the parameter passed. In this case, this will be the delimiter. Observe the example in Example 8-2.

Example 8-2. Split example 1

```
1 my_string = "Good;day;sir!"
2 arr = my_string.split(";")
3 puts arr
4
5 # The following array is created:
6 # arr[0]: "Good"
7 # arr[1]: "day"
8 # arr[2]: "sir!"
```

- Line 1 defines a string object with the value "Good;day;sir!"
- Line 2 calls the built-in method split with a semicolon as the parameter.
- Line 3 outputs the values of my_array.

After executing the code, the array shown in lines 6–8 will be created, and the output will be the following:

```
$ ruby split_1.rb
Good
day
sir!
```

As you can see, the split method has created an array with three indices based on the parameter passed (in this case, the semicolon). Now, what if we changed the parameter of the split method to something else, as shown in Example 8-3?

Example 8-3. Split example 2

```
1 my_string = "Good;day;sir!"
2 arr = my_string.split("a")
3 puts arr
4
5 # The following array is created:
6 # arr[0]: "Good;d"
7 # arr[1]: "y;sir!"
```

Now the `split` method will perform the same operation, but instead of splitting the string object based on the semicolon, it will split the string into array values based on the new parameter. The resultant array is once again shown in the comments in lines 6 and 7, with the following output:

```
$ ruby split_2.rb
Good;d
y;sir!
```

The `split` method has created an array with two elements based on the parameter a. You can see that no matter what the input is, the program will always perform the same operation based on the parameter passed. It does not matter what the input is or what is inside the method; the `split` method will create arrays splitting your string object wherever there is an occurrence of the indicated parameter.

An astute reader may wonder what would happen if the chosen parameter for `split` did not exist in the string, `my_string`. In this case, an array of one element is returned, with the first element containing `my_string`. The code in Example 8-4 illustrates this.

The output follows from the array's structure, as shown in line 6.

Example 8-4. Split example 3

```
1 my_string = "Good;day;sir!"
2 arr = my_string.split("z")
3 puts arr
4
5 # The following array is created:
6 # arr[0]: "Good;day;sir!"

$ ruby split_3.rb
Good;day;sir!
```

8.3 Summary

Objects and their corresponding methods are the building blocks of many of today's software systems. For all object-oriented programming languages, some objects and methods are predefined, and those are always specified in the language manuals.

In that light, we introduced objects, explained built-in objects, and discussed parameter passing, a mechanism to transfer information in and out of objects.

8.3.1 Key Concepts

- *Classes* define the characteristics and behaviors of objects belonging to the class.
- *Objects* are instantiations of a class. They have a name and possess all the properties of the class, namely, the variables and the methods.
- The *application user interface*, or *API*, is an interface used to communicate with some underlying functionality.

8.3.2 Key Definitions

- *Object*: An isolated piece of code that has its own actions and data.
- *Method*: The action that an object may perform.
- *API*: An interface provided to the programmer to allow the use of certain functionality without knowing the specifics of the implementation.
- *Class*: Construct that contains the definition of an object template and the implementation of the methods.
- *Parameter passing*: The passing of data to a method within an object.

8.4 Exercises

1. Provide code using the `split` method to separate the following string into individual words and then display them:

    ```
    my_string = "Roses!are!red!Violets!are!blue"
    ```

2. You are programming part of the sign-up procedure for an online computer game. Write a program that prompts the user to enter his or her user ID and password and enforces the following restrictions:

    a. User IDs and passwords must be *at least* seven characters in length.

    b. Passwords must contain *at least* one of each of the following: uppercase character, lowercase character, number, and symbol.

    Hint: use the documentation for the string class.

3. Write a program that prompts the user for three words and then outputs the total and average number of characters in the three words.

4. What would result if you were to type the following into irb?

```
irb(main):001:0> "12345".length
irb(main):002:0> "12345" * 5
irb(main):003:0> "12345".index(2)
irb(main):004:0> "12345".index(0)
irb(main):005:0> "12345".index(1)
irb(main):006:0> "12345".index(5)
```

5. What does it mean to pass a parameter to a method? What happens when a parameter is passed to a method?

6. Write a function multiplier that multiplies the value passed to it by x. Have the function ask the user for the value of x.

CHAPTER 9

Defining Classes and Creating Objects

In This Chapter

- Instantiating objects from classes
- Data and methods in objects

9.1 Introduction

The preceding chapter introduced classes and objects and some of the vocabulary associated with objects. It also delved into a few of the built-in objects within Ruby. Now it is time to explore the true power of objects: the ability to create your own.

9.2 Instantiating Objects from Classes

As we mentioned in previous chapters, a class is a description of objects. A particular object is an instantiation of the class, having a unique name selected for it by the programmers. As with all information in a computer system, the various classes are stored in files. When reading the previous chapters, you probably noticed the following syntax in some examples:

```
customer = String.new
```

This is essentially the syntax for instantiating a new object. The example shows that you are instantiating an object whose class is `String`. The object's name is `customer`, and the name is used as a variable from the class `String`. Now you can manipulate the `customer` variable using the different methods learned in the preceding chapters.

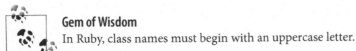

Gem of Wisdom

In Ruby, class names must begin with an uppercase letter.

Ruby provides many built-in classes like strings and arrays, but you can also create your own class. User-defined classes are a great way to group and categorize something's characteristics. For example, if you want to organize a database for bank accounts, you can create a class describing the properties and behaviors of each bank account.

Example 9-1 provides an outline for defining your own class.

Example 9-1. Class definition syntax

```
 1 class Classname
 2  def initialize(var1, var2, ..., varn)
 3    @variable_1 = var1
 4    @variable_2 = var2
 5    ...
 6    @variable_n = varn
 7  end
 8
 9  def method_1
10    # code
11  end
12
13  def method_2
14    # code
15  end
16 end
```

We now describe lines 1–7 (the rest will be covered in the following sections), which define a class and initialize variables local to the class. To define a class, use the `class` keyword followed by a descriptive name that characterizes an object. For example, if you wanted to create a class for a bank account called `Account`, define the class by typing:

```
class Account
end
```

Another important keyword you should notice in the class definition is `def` (short for define). This keyword is used to define new activities (called *methods*) that may be performed on the object. This keyword is also used to define the special method `initialize`, which is called every time a new instance of the class, that is, a new object, is created. All classes have this special method, which is called a *constructor*. We will explain class generation using an example of a class describing bank accounts called `Account`, the first iteration of which can be seen in Example 9-2.

Gem of Wisdom

Each created instance of a class will have its own unique instance variables. If a variable is prefixed with @@, it becomes a class variable that is *shared* across *all* instances of the class. We do not discuss class variables in this book.

Example 9-2. Account version 1

```
1 class Account
2   def initialize(balance)
3     @balance = balance
4   end
5 end
```

The variables inside the parentheses after `initialize` are the parameters that are assigned when creating, or instantiating, the object.

Now when instantiating an object using the `Account` class, the object will have a variable called `balance` with an initial value that you can assign using a parameter. The special character (@) is used to indicate that this is an *instance variable*, meaning that it is a parameter of the object. Variables might be specific to a single method in the class, but these instance variables can be accessed by any method in the object description. These instance variables are sometimes referred to *as storing the properties of an object*.

We have just created a user-defined class, but how do you use it? You can instantiate an object of the `Account` class the same way you create new strings and arrays:

```
bob = Account.new(10.00)
```

This example creates an object called `bob` of the `Account` class. Remember when you created the `initialize` method? You assigned one parameter called `balance`; this is the value in the parentheses. The parameter passed in the parentheses will become the initial balance of Bob's account.

What other variables should you consider adding to the `Account` class? What kind of behaviors should the class contain? In the following sections, we describe grouping data, as well as adding your own methods and working with the data through the object's methods.

9.3 Data and Methods

Objects are made up of two important concepts: the data the object holds (the instance variables) and the actions the object can perform (the methods).

Gem of Wisdom

Note that the instance variables `balance`, `name`, and `phone_number` are assigned in the order the parameters were passed to the `initialize` method; however, this is not required. It is done merely for convenience to the reader. Also, the actual names can be chosen arbitrarily. For example, `@cash = balance`, while allowed, is discouraged.

9.3.1 Grouping Data and Methods

The previous section detailed how to create and instantiate an object of an `Account` class, and while reading it you might have been thinking to yourself, "How was I supposed to know that an `Account` class needs a `balance` variable?" The answer is that no class requires any particular piece of data, but classes are used to group related pieces of data together, and it only makes sense that an account has a balance. Likewise, there are other things that would come as a part of a bank account. Depending on the nature of the bank account, the type of data included would change. For example, a savings account wouldn't necessarily include the same data as a checking account. Regardless, we are talking about a generic bank account, and additional data possibly included are name, phone number, Social Security number, minimum balance, and maximum balance. We now introduce two additional instance variables to our `Account` class, as shown in Example 9-3.

Example 9-3. Account version 2

```
1 class Account
2   def initialize(balance, name, phone_number)
3     @balance = balance
4     @name = name
5     @phone_number = phone_number
6   end
7 end
```

Our bank account is beginning to make a bit more sense. On top of just having a balance, there is a name and a phone number attached to the account, so we can uniquely determine whose account it is. Now that our `Account` class constructor has changed, let's see how to initialize Bob's bank account when he has $10 as his starting balance, and has a phone number of 716-634-9483.

```
bob = Account.new(10.00, "Bob", 7166349483)
```

An object also contains methods. Just like data, methods are logically grouped together based on the class. The purpose of a method is to accomplish a task, so we must ask ourselves, what actions should a bank account have? We would expect that at the very least we could withdraw from and deposit to our account. Let's add these methods to our `Account` class, as shown in Example 9-4.

Example 9-4. Account version 3

```
 1 class Account
 2  def initialize(balance, name, phone_number)
 3   @balance = balance
 4   @name = name
 5   @phone_number = phone_number
 6  end
 7
 8  def deposit(amount)
 9   # code
10  end
11
12  def withdraw(amount)
13   # code
14  end
15 end
```

Aside from the missing implementation code on lines 9 and 13, our Account class implementation is looking pretty good. Not only can Bob open an account, but he can also deposit or withdraw money when he desires.

The Account class is almost finished, and the only thing left to do before Bob is able to open a bank account is to implement the deposit and withdraw methods.

9.3.2 Implementing Methods

A key advantage of objects is that they abstract the details of their operations away from the code that uses them. Once the details of the Account class are finalized, a programmer can use the class without knowing any of those details. The programmer need only know what data are required to initialize the class, and what data are required for each method in the class. For example, consider the String class provided in the Ruby standard library. When we use the capitalize method, we do not know how String stores the data, nor how the data get accessed. All we need to know is that the capitalize method capitalizes the first letter of the string.

As we implement an object, we must consider every detail of its operation. The deposit method, for example, must add the value of the parameter passed to the previous @balance and store the result back in @balance. Let's take a look at the implementation of the deposit and withdraw methods, as shown in Example 9-5.

Gem of Wisdom

Recalling our earlier Gem of Wisdom and looking at Example 9-5, using our shorthand construct known as op=, in line 9, the variable @balance is incremented by the value of amount, meaning @balance = @balance + amount, and in line 13, the meaning of the statement is @balance = @balance - amount.

Example 9-5. Account version 4

```
1 class Account
2  def initialize(balance, name, phone_number)
3    @balance = balance
4    @name = name
5    @phone_number = phone_number
6  end
7
8  def deposit(amount)
9    @balance += amount
10 end
11
12 def withdraw(amount)
13   @balance -= amount
14 end
15 end
```

To use these newly defined methods, we must initialize the classes and then access them as we did with built-in methods. Note in the following code that this is the first time we import definitions using the require command. For example, to create an account for Mary, with $500, and then to deposit another $200, we would perform the following steps in irb:

```
irb(main):003:0> require 'account_4.rb'
=> true
irb(main):004:0> mary_account = Account.new(500, "Mary", 8181000000)
=> #<Account:0x3dfa68 @balance=500, @name="Mary", @phone_number=8181000000>
irb(main):005:0> mary_account.deposit(200)
=> 700
irb(main):006:0> mary_account
=> #<Account:0x3dfa68 @balance=700, @name="Mary", @phone_number=8181000000>
```

As can be seen from the output, Mary's account now holds 700 in its @balance variable. However, it would be much nicer to provide a helper method to display this information. The display method is an often-used method for outputting the contents of an object's instance. For the Account class, we can output the name, phone number, and account balance to the screen with the code shown in Example 9-6.

Example 9-6. Display method

```
1 def display()
2   puts "Name: " + @name
3   puts "Phone Number: " + @phone_number.to_s
4   puts "Balance: " + @balance.to_s
5 end
```

Now we can immediately see the result of our actions. For example, try running the following code, which indirectly transfers $200 from Bob's account to Mary's:

```
bob_account = Account.new(500, "Bob", 8181000000)
mary_account = Account.new(500, "Mary", 8881234567)
bob_account.withdraw(200)
mary_account.deposit(200)
bob_account.display()
mary_account.display()
```

Note that in both the method definition in Example 9-6 and in its use in the preceding code, empty parentheses are included. Such use is optional; however, we include it to reinforce the fact that parameters are needed.

At the end of executing those instructions, bob_account would have $300 as its balance, and mary_account would have $700. However, every time we would want to use the Account class to transfer money, we would have to write two lines: one for withdrawing from the old account and another for depositing to a new one. It would be much easier to use the Account class if the two functionalities were combined into a single method. This single method would need to affect two separate instances of a single class. This is done by passing an account object to a new method called transfer, shown in Example 9-7.

Example 9-7. Transfer method

```
1 def transfer(amount, target_account)
2   @balance -= amount
3   target_account.deposit(amount)
4 end
```

Finally, all our methods thus far affected values stored in the program.

However, none of our defined methods returned a value to the invoking statement. That is, if one wished to assign the balance of an account to a variable, this balance would need to be returned after a sequence of deposits and withdrawals. To obtain this value, a method must be defined that returns a value. We define such a method, called status, as shown in Example 9-8.

Example 9-8. Status method

```
1 def status
2   return @balance
3 end
```

Two items are critical to note about the definition of the status method. First, the return construct returns the value of @balance to the method-invoking element. For the sophisticated Ruby programmer, the reality is that Ruby always returns the value of the last statement executed. However, if a different value or better clarity is desired, a return statement is often used.

Second, since there is no local overriding parameter called @balance, the global value for @balance is accessed. Example 9-9 contains the full implementation of our Account class.

Example 9-9. Account—final version (version 5)

```
 1 class Account
 2   def initialize(balance, name, phone_number)
 3     @balance = balance
 4     @name = name
 5     @phone_number = phone_number
 6   end
 7
 8   def deposit(amount)
 9     @balance += amount
10   end
11
12   def withdraw(amount)
13     @balance -= amount
14   end
15
16   def display
17     puts "Name: " + @name
18     puts "Phone number: " + @phone_number.to_s
19     puts "Balance: " + @balance.to_s
20   end
21
22   def transfer(amount, target_account)
23     @balance -= amount
24     target_account.deposit(amount)
25   end
26
27   def status
28     return @balance
29   end
30 end
```

9.4 Summary

We described how to create objects and methods. The special method initialize was discussed as the means to implement a constructor. Also, class variables were described.

9.4.1 Key Concepts

- *Objects* are created by *instantiation*. This is done via the *constructor* contained in the class definition.

- When creating a class, it is important to keep in mind that objects from the class are meant to group data and methods together.

- A key point to keep in mind when working with objects is that once an object has been created, it abstracts the details away from the program that uses it. In other words, you can use an object without seeing the details of that object directly.

9.4.2 Key Definitions

- *Instantiating objects from classes*: The creation of new objects.

- *Constructor*: A special method that all classes have that initializes the data in an object each time a new object is created.

- *Instance variable*: A variable that is unique to an instance of a class. It stores information relevant to the object.

9.5 Exercises

1. Create two classes to represent the following two objects: televisions and speakers. Include an `initialize` function and several methods to interact with your objects.

2. Given two Cartesian points (x_1, y_1) and (x_2, y_2), the slope of the line segment connecting them is given by the formula $(y_2 - y_1)/(x_2 - x_1)$.

    Write a class that represents a Cartesian point. Define a method `find_slope` that takes in a Cartesian point object and finds the slope between the two points. Test your class with the following:

    a. (0,0) (3,4)

    b. (2,3) (6,5)

    c. (2,2) (2,7)

    What happens in the last case? Why does that happen?

3. Define a class that compares two numbers and outputs the larger one. Test your solution.

4. Briefly explain the code illustrated in Example 9-10.

Example 9-10. Code for Exercise 4

```
1 class Profile
2  def initialize(name, phone_number)
3    @name = name
4    @phone_number = phone_number
5  end
6
7  def display
8    puts "Name ==> " + @name
9    puts "Phone number ==> " + @phone_number.to_s
10 end
11 end
```

5. Write a `Student` class that contains a student's name, gender, phone number, and exam score. It should also include the `initialize`, `accumulated_score`, and `display` methods.

CHAPTER 10

Object Inheritance

In This Chapter

- Inheritance
- Overriding methods
- Accessing the superclass
- Applications of inheritance

10.1 Introduction

The preceding two chapters introduced you to the use and creation of simple objects. Now it is time to show how objects can be created from other objects. This chapter covers inheritance, method overriding, and various applications of objects.

10.2 Inheritance

At this point in the book, your programming style is starting to become more sophisticated. No longer are you writing code where one long file encompasses everything you do. Now you are using objects, and you are also beginning to program in an object-oriented manner. Object-oriented programming (OOP) is a powerful form of programming that is currently extremely popular and the backbone for many new languages, including Ruby.

Thus far, we have talked about creating simple objects that are independent of one another. However, one of the most powerful abilities OOP has is the ability to define relationships between objects. The first of these relationships is known as *inheritance*. To understand the concept of inheritance, imagine a ball (any spherical object that could

Gem of Wisdom

Object inheritance is one of the most powerful parts of object-oriented pro-gramming. Inheritance enables hierarchical decomposition of structures into logically encapsulated units.

pass for a ball will do). Perhaps you are thinking of a baseball, a tennis ball, or a ping-pong ball; it does not matter which because all those balls have a large degree of similarity among them, despite being different types of balls or even different objects. If we needed to accomplish some task and asked you for a ball, they could all work despite their differences. Inheritance allows us to define these types of relationships with Ruby ob-jects. This ends up saving the programmer significant time and code because she or he need not redefine parts of the objects that are similar.

Let's return to our bank account example from the preceding chapter. It defined what is essentially a checking account, and our bank is no longer happy with just this one type of account; now it wants to expand to include savings accounts. The first thing to notice are the similarities between a savings account and a checking account: they both maintain a balance and can have money withdrawn from them and deposited to them. The class that defines the similarities in the relationship is referred to as the parent class, or the *superclass*.

The main differences between the two bank accounts are that you cannot withdraw beyond the minimum balance from a savings account (we will touch on this in the next section) and that a savings account generates interest. The class that defines the differ-ences in the relationship is referred to as the child class or the *subclass*. Now we will use inheritance to define this `SavingsAccount` class (see Example 10-1).

Example 10-1. SavingsAccount version 1

```
 1 require_relative '../chapter_09/account_5.rb'
 2
 3 class SavingsAccount < Account
 4   def initialize(balance, name, phone_number, interest, minimum)
 5     super(balance, name, phone_number)
 6     @interest = interest
 7     @minimum = minimum
 8   end
 9
10   def accumulate_interest
11     @balance += @balance * @interest
12   end
13 end
```

Note that we use the `require_relative` command instead of the `require` command. `require` loads files that are installed as Ruby libraries or files for which the full path to the file is given. `require_relative` is used to load files without specifying the full path to the file; it looks for files in a location relative to the file `require_relative` is used in.

The first thing to note in the code provided in Example 10-1 is the < symbol (on line 3). This is the symbol used to define inheritance in Ruby. In this case, the parent class is the `Account` class, which is predefined via line 1, and the child class is the `SavingsAccount` class. See the account class in Example 9-9.

The next thing to look over is the constructor of the `SavingsAccount` class, expressed by the `initialize` method on line 4. Immediately, in line 5, this method calls a method named `super()`, which is the equivalent of calling the `initialize` method for the superclass `Account`. After this, we initialize the instance variables `@interest` and `@minimum`. It is important to note that these pieces of data distinguish a `SavingsAccount` from a `CheckingAccount` and the subclass from the superclass.

Finally, there is the `accumulate_interest` method, which is just a simple interest calculation.

However, thanks to inheritance, the `SavingsAccount` class can do more than just accumulate interest. It also inherits all the data and methods from the `Account` class. Table 10-1 is a summary of everything inherited by the `SavingsAccount` class.

Table 10-1. SavingsAccount inherited summary

Data	Methods
@balance	withdraw(amount)
@name	deposit(amount)
@phone_number	transfer(amount, targetAccount)
	display

If we create an instance of the `SavingsAccount` class:

```
account = SavingsAccount.new(200.00, "Reynolds",
9694905555, 0.015, 150)
```

we can then call any of the following methods:

```
account.deposit(amount)
account.withdraw(amount)
account.transfer(amount, targetAccount)
account.accumulate_interest
account.display
```

This explicitly shows the power of inheritance. Although we never defined four of the five methods shown for the SavingsAccount class, we can use them because they are inherited from the parent class, Account. The SavingsAccount class consists of only 11 lines of code, but it has as much functionality as 41 lines of code (the number of lines of code in Example 10-1 plus Example 9-9).

If we were to return to the transfer(amount, targetAccount) method from the preceding chapter we would see that it was designed to transfer money from one account to another. At the time we created the method, we had not designed a SavingsAccount and were content with it working only on Account objects. However, it will work on SavingsAccount objects, because a SavingsAccount is an Account; it has enough similarity for a transfer between accounts to be possible. This is another powerful ability granted by inheritance, and it is known as *polymorphism*. Polymorphism, however, does not work both ways. With the transfer(amount, targetAccount) method example, the polymorphism is from the subclass to the superclass. Polymorphism will not work when you are trying to morph from a superclass to a subclass, because the subclass has abilities the superclass does not. To express this in an example, imagine trying to call the accumulate_interest() method from an Account object; it won't work because only SavingsAccount objects, not Account objects, have the accumulate_interest() method.

10.3 Basic Method Overriding

When extending a class, it is sometimes convenient to alter methods that already exist in the class's superclass. For example, both the checking and saving accounts need a method for withdrawing money. However, the methods are only the same on the outside. Unlike the regular checking account, the savings account needs to check if the balance would fall below the minimum allowed. To achieve this, the SavingsAccount class will need to override the withdraw method by defining its own withdraw functionality, as shown in Example 10-2. Overriding is accomplished by using the same name in the local class. The local definition always supersedes the parent definition.

Example 10-2. SavingsAccount version 2

```ruby
 1 require_relative '../chapter_09/account_5.rb'
 2
 3 class SavingsAccount < Account
 4   def initialize(balance, name, phone_number, interest, minimum)
 5     super(balance, name, phone_number)
 6     @interest = interest
 7     @minimum = minimum
 8   end
 9
10   def accumulate_interest
11     @balance += @balance * @interest
12   end
13
14   def withdraw(amount)
15     if (@balance - amount >= @minimum)
16       @balance -= amount
17     else
18       puts "Balance cannot drop below: " + @minimum.to_s
19     end
20   end
21 end
```

Instead of calling on the withdraw method that belongs to Account, the SavingsAccount class will use the new withdraw method that overrode it. As a result, any instances of SavingsAccount will not be able to fall below their minimum account balances. This powerful property of OOP has its problems. It implies that the writer of a subclass be fully cognizant of the methods and instance variables of the superclass.

10.4 Accessing the Superclass

In many cases, the overriding methods will have similar functionality to the methods they override. It is counterproductive to the concept of inheritance to just rewrite the same methods again with slightly altered code. Inheritance exists to make code reuse as easy as possible. As such, it provides a way to avoid rewriting the superclass method. Simply insert the word super with all the parameters that would be used to call the superclass method bearing the same name wherever you would like the superclass's method, just like the initialize method. Applying this to our new SavingsAccount class, we get the code in Example 10-3.

Example 10-3. SavingsAccount version 3

```
 1 require_relative '../chapter_09/account_5.rb'
 2
 3 class SavingsAccount < Account
 4  def initialize(balance, name, phone_number, interest, minimum)
 5   super(balance, name, phone_number)
 6   @interest = interest
 7   @minimum = minimum
 8  end
 9
10  def accumulate_interest
11   @balance += @balance * @interest
12  end
13
14  def withdraw(amount)
15   if (@balance - amount >= @minimum)
16    super(amount)
17   else
18    puts "Balance cannot drop below: " + @minimum.to_s
19   end
20  end
21 end
```

In our example, obviously the benefits seem minimal. However, for complex programs, the advantages of using predefined classes are tremendous. Not only are we saving ourselves the time of rewriting the class, but we are also making code maintenance easier. If the `withdraw` method needs to be updated, we can update it in the `Account` class. Any subclasses that use it as their superclass will be updated accordingly, wherever they have called `super`.

10.5 Applications

Inheritance is a way to form new classes that borrow attributes and behaviors of previously defined classes. After learning about inheritance and method overriding, you are probably wondering when you will ever need to use them. What is the big deal about inheritance? Why can't we just make a bunch of different classes? To put it simply, it saves significant unnecessary coding by eliminating code duplication, and it simplifies software testing and maintenance since functionality and local data are isolated. Here are several other examples for which you can use inheritance.

10.5.1 Person Database

A contractor is looking for a way to keep track of all the people in his organization. He has full-time and part-time employees, student interns, and volunteers. In this example, you can make a class called `Person`. This class can have the individual's name, address, phone number, email address, and weekly hours worked. You can have a method called email that emails all the employees to remind them to turn in their time sheets. Then you can have subclasses called Full, Part, Intern, and Volunteer. For the Full subclass, you can include variables like hourly wage and overtime pay. For a behavior you can have a process_payment method to deposit money into the employee's bank account. A student Intern would have different variables. Maybe you want to keep track of who has the highest grade-point average or test scores to see which one is the top intern. Thus, you would create some variables for the aforementioned categories. For members of the Volunteer subclass, you probably would not want to send them an email about turning in their time sheets to get paid, so you should make a custom method that asks them how many hours they volunteered. You can create an email method that overrides the previous one.

10.5.2 Grocery Store

You go to a small grocery store and overhear the owner complaining about keeping track of his food. He orders food every week, but his employees have no idea what to do with the food when it comes in. You can create a database program with a class called Food. This class can have variables like the name of the item, the price, and the location where it is stored. You can have a method called PrintLabel to create price labels to stick on the food. Possible subclasses to consider are Fruit, Meat, and Grain. Most of the foods will have traits in common, so you won't need to worry about creating too many variables. The PrintLabel method will create tiny stickers you can put on the food, but what if you had a Fruit like raisins or grapes? There is no possible way you can print labels to stick on each individual fruit. You will probably want to use method overriding to print bigger labels you can stick on the shelf near the respective fruit.

10.5.3 Video Games

You have been hired to create a role-playing video game called "Pirates and Ninjas of the Pacific," where players can choose to play as ninjas or pirates. How are you going to keep track of all the players' characters? You can create a class called Player with variables for name, health points, and experience. You should also include methods for walking and fighting so that the player can move around and kill monsters by fighting with them. Since pirates and ninjas obviously have different skills, you will probably want to create subclasses called Pirate and Ninja. Ninjas generally fight using hand-to-hand combat; so you would not need to change their Fight method. Pirates, on the other hand, generally lack hand-to-hand combat skills and use guns instead. What's the solution? Override their Fight method with something that allows them to shoot guns. But ninjas don't always just fight with their hands, so you could create additional methods like throw and jump.

Looking at this and the preceding examples, you can get the general idea for when classes, inheritance, and method overriding can be useful. These techniques are used in every field of computer science. You can implement inheritance whether you are programming for a contractor, a grocer, or a video game company. As an exercise, try to come up with three of your own examples for which you can use classes, inheritance, and method overriding.

10.6 Summary

We have introduced the notion of object inheritance and shown some examples.

10.6.1 Key Concepts

- One of the most powerful tools in *object-oriented programming* (OOP) is that objects can be created from other objects and use the resources of the parent object. This is known as *inheritance*. In this relationship, the parent class or superclass defines the relationship with the child class or subclass.
- *Subclasses* inherit both data and methods from their *parent class*.
- A key point to keep in mind when working with inheritance is that *polymorphism* often takes place, which in some cases can lead to a need for method overriding.

10.6.2 Key Definitions

- *Inheritance*: When the relationship between two classes is defined.
- *Superclass*: The class that defines the object for the relationship.
- *Subclass*: The class for which the relationship is defined.
- *Method overriding*: When the method for a parent class is redefined for a child class.
- *Polymorphism*: Allows different data types to be handled by a unified interface.

10.7 Exercises

1. The class shown in Example 10-4 is used to keep track of the inventory for a company. It allows the user to assign a name and a manufacturer to each item. Write a class ItemNumber that inherits from Item that lets the user input a number of items owned for each item. Create an instance of the Item class and then an instance of the ItemNumber class.

Example 10-4. Code for Exercise 1

```
 1 class Item
 2 def initialize(item, maker)
 3   @item = item
 4   @maker = maker
 5 end
 6
 7 def display
 8   puts "Item ==> " + @item
 9   puts "Maker ==> " + @maker
10 end
11 end
```

2. Explain polymorphism.

3. Define OOP.

4. A university has three kinds of students: full-time students, part-time students, and off-campus students. Each student has the following information: name, address, phone number, Social Security number, student ID, and GPA. The full-time students should take at least 12 credits per semester. The part-time students should take less than 12 credits per semester. The off-campus students have no limit on credits per semester. The tuition fee for full-time students is $8,500 for up to 18 credits per semester and $600 for every credit over 18 credits. The tuition fee for part-time students is $750 per credit. The tuition fee for off-campus students is $520 per credit. Write a program that lists student information and calculates their tuition fees.

5. Write a program for the grocery store example described in Section 10.5.2, "Grocery Store."

CHAPTER 11

File Input/Output

In This Chapter

- Reading files
- Writing files

11.1 Introduction

Until this point, all of our programs have taken a data set of values from user input. Any given program took in one data set, which consisted of one or more related values from the user, and then performed a computation based on that data set. Imagine a program that has many data sets, each consisting of multiple values. Entering all the data sets by hand could be somewhat time-consuming. Also, some data sets may come from external sources and not directly from the user.

The techniques presented in this chapter will allow you to manipulate files and utilize their data within your software. File input/output (I/O) allows software to perform computations on sets of data until a desired end result is achieved.

11.2 File Access: Reading and Writing

To access files, the built-in Ruby File class is used. This class contains multiple methods. We use the following: open, close, gets, and puts. The method File.open instantiates a new object that enables Ruby to read from or write to an existing or new file. The object returned by File.open can then be used by Ruby to access the file. The following code shows how to open a file:

```
myfile = File.open(file_name, access_mode)
```

Gem of Wisdom

Files provide access to data resident in the computer system's long-term memory. Storage in long-term memory, such as disks, provides data resiliency, namely, permanence. That is, disks work even without power, so they store things far longer than the internal random access memory, which works only if the power is on.

The `myfile` variable is a `File` object that can now be used to interact with the file's contents, depending on what access mode is used. Note that `file name` and `access mode` are strings. The variable `file_name` is a representation of a path to a file, such as */home/ruby/file.txt*. The `myfile` variable in our program is local to only our program. Two of the most basic access modes and what they do are shown in Table 11-1.

Table 11-1. Some file access modes

Mode	Description
r	Read access only. Points to start of the file. This is the default, but it is good programming style to specify it anyway.
w	Write access only. Points to the beginning of the file that will overwrite the file's content if it already exists.

To read a line of characters from a file, call the `gets` method on the `myfile` object. When the `gets` method is called, it reads characters until it reaches a newline character (\n), and then it returns what it read. The `File` object keeps track of what has been read in, so each successive call to `gets` will always return the next line, until it reaches the end of the file and returns `nil`. `nil` has the logical truth value of `false`. Every other value returned by `gets` has the logical value of `true`. Consider the code provided in Example 11-1, which reads in a file *foo.txt* and then prints it out.

Example 11-1. Sample code for file reading

```
 1 myfile = File.open("foo.txt", "r")
 2 whole_file = ""
 3
 4 while (input_line = myfile.gets)
 5   whole_file += input_line
 6 end
 7
 8 puts "Contents of input file:"
 9 puts whole_file
10 myfile.close()
```

- Line 1 opens *foo.txt* for read access.

- Line 2 instantiates an empty string variable, `whole_file`, which will be used to store the file to display.

- Lines 4–6 contain a loop that reads the file into `input_line`, one line at a time, and appends each line into `whole_file`.

- Line 9 prints out the file.

Sequentially writing to a file is similar to sequentially reading from a file. Instead of opening the file in read mode, the file needs to be opened with w for writing access. To write text to a file, use the local variable myfile to call the puts method:

```
myfile.puts("text goes here!")
```

The code shown in Example 11-2 opens a file for write access, accepts user input, and writes that input to the file. It will then close the file, reopen it, and print the contents to verify correctness.

Example 11-2. File read/write example

```
 1 file_a = File.open("bar.txt", "w")
 2
 3 puts "Please enter a line of text"
 4 line = gets()
 5 file_a.puts(line)
 6 file_a.close()
 7
 8 file_b = File.open("bar.txt", "r")
 9 puts "Contents of file:"
10 puts file_b.gets()
11 file_b.close()
```

- Line 1 opens *bar.txt* as file object file_a with write access.
- Lines 3–4 take text input from the user.
- Line 5 writes the user input into "bar.txt".
- Line 6 closes the File object file_a (this saves the text inside it by closing the file and preventing further access to it).
- Line 8 instantiates a new File object file_b. This object will be used for the purpose of reading the content of *bar.txt*. Note the file access mode r.
- Line 10 outputs the contents of the newly created file to the console, illustrating that the code in Example 11-2 behaves in the desired fashion.

11.2.1 File Reader Class

We will now define two classes that encapsulate reading in a file and writing out a file. Then we will use the two classes to create a file copy program that will read text from a file and then copy the text into a new file.

The class presented in Example 11-3 encapsulates reading and displaying a file.

Example 11-3. FileReader class

```
 1 class FileReader
 2
 3  def initialize(file_name)
 4    @file = File.open(file_name, "r")
 5  end
 6
 7  def read_file
 8    whole_file = ""
 9    while (input_line = @file.gets)
10      whole_file += input_line
11    end
12
13    return whole_file
14  end
15
16  def display
17    puts "Contents of input file:"
18    puts read_file
19  end
20
21  def close
22    @file.close()
23  end
24 end
```

- Lines 3–5 define the constructor. The variable @file references the File object that has been opened.

- Line 4 opens the file for the purpose of reading the contents. The r indicates that this file is to be open for reading.

- Lines 7–14 define the read file method. This method incorporates a basic loop that goes through a given file using gets for the purpose of reading one line at a time.

- Line 10 appends (adds to the end of the string) to whole_file the contents of the currently read line of the file.

- Line 13 returns the contents of the file that is now stored in whole_file.

- Lines 16–19 define a display method that outputs the contents of the file.

- Lines 21–23 define a close method that closes the opened file, @file.

11.2.2 FileWriter Class

The class in Example 11-4 encapsulates writing to and closing a file.

Example 11-4. FileWriter class

```
1 class FileWriter
2
3   def initialize(file_name)
4     @file = File.open(file_name, "w")
5   end
6
7   def write_line(output_line)
8     @file.puts(output_line)
9   end
10
11   def close
12     @file.close()
13   end
14 end
```

- Lines 3–5 define the constructor.
- Line 4 opens the file `file_name` using `w` for write access mode.
- Lines 7–9 define the `write_line` method, which outputs a single line, `output_line`, to a file associated with the `FileWriter` object.
- Line 8 makes use of the `puts` method to output the contents of a given `output_line` to the file referenced by `@file`.
- Lines 11–13 close the file. This ensures that all the data that have been written to the file are actually written to it. That is, data that are temporarily buffered in intermediate storage are actually written to secondary (permanent) storage. Buffering is commonly used to reduce output writing delays.

The above use of buffers may seem obscure for a reader who is not familiar with the actual mechanisms employed in writing a file. In reality, the `puts` method does not actually write to a file; it actually fills a holding area commonly referred to as a buffer.

11.2.3 File Reader/Writer Example

The code in Example 11-5 will read in a file and write the contents out to a new file. This code assumes you have written out the class definitions for `FileReader` and `FileWriter` given in the preceding section as files named *file_reader.rb* and *file_writer.rb*.

Example 11-5. FileReader/FileWriter example

```
 1 require_relative "file_reader.rb"
 2 require_relative "file_writer.rb"
 3
 4 fr = FileReader.new("input.txt")
 5 fw = FileWriter.new("output.txt")
 6
 7 input = fr.read_file()
 8 fw.write_line(input)
 9
10 fw.close()
11 fr.close()
```

- Lines 1 and 2 import the class definitions of `FileReader` and `FileWriter`.
- Lines 4 and 5 create instances of our two classes, the first for input, the second for output.
- Line 7 reads the file into a string called `input`.
- Line 8 writes the string `input` out to the file held by the instance of `FileWriter`.
- Lines 10 and 11 close both of the open files.

To verify that the code presented in Example 11-5 works correctly, use the input text file with the content shown in Example 11-6. After running Example 11-5's code with the input from Example 11-6, ensure that *output.txt* is the same as *input.txt*.

Example 11-6. Sample input file

```
Hello world!
A mighty fine day for ruby programming!
Computer Science is the best!
```

11.3 Summary

We described basic file input and output operations.

11.3.1 Key Concepts

- Text files in Ruby are contiguous streams of data in the form of characters.
- Data can be entered into a program using *file access*; this is done through file *input/output* or I/O.
- To read from or write to a file, one must access the file through Ruby's `File` class.

11.3.2 Key Definitions

- *File access*: Opening a file for reading or writing.
- *Input*: Reading information from a stored file.
- *Output*: Writing information to a file for storage.

11.4 Exercises

1. The game of Go is often played online. Many users save their game data for later analysis. The game is played by two players who take turns placing stones (one player using black stones and the other using white stones) on the intersections of a 19 × 19 board. Create a program to enter each move of a game and save that information to a file.

2. Write a program that quizzes the user on her or his vocabulary. Make the program read a set of words and definitions from a file; display definitions one at a time, in random order; and prompt for the appropriate word.

3. Write a program that will keep track of the mileage for oil changes for your car.

4. Write a program that reads the content of a file and outputs it to the screen.

5. Write a program that takes input from the user and saves it to a file.

6. Write a program that creates and stores a simple address book.

CHAPTER 12

Putting It All Together: Tic-Tac-Toe

In This Chapter

- Approaching the problem
- Implementing tic-tac-toe

12.1 Introduction

It is finally time to put everything you know all together. You will no longer use programming elements in isolation; writing programs rarely involves using only if statements, loops, or objects. Typically, all programming elements are interleaved. For clarity, we described these elements in isolation; now we integrate them. The challenge is to create a task that requires integration that is not too simple to be uninteresting but not so complex that it requires 500 pages of text.

After much thought, we decided to develop the simple, well-known game of tic-tac-toe. The idea is to initially develop a program that facilitates two people playing against each other, and then to enhance the program so that a person can play against a computer. As correct play guarantees at least a tie, we provide sufficient algorithm detail to guarantee that the computer will never lose. We provide sufficient code segments to illustrate the development of the program but leave it to you to complete it. Good luck; you are ready for it.

Using what you have learned so far, it is time to put all of your knowledge together into one fun program. The game of tic-tac-toe is a classic, and the rules can be easily looked up if you are not familiar with them. First you will learn how to build a Ruby program that will allow two users to play the game. After this program has been established, we will extend the program to allow a user to play against the computer.

Gem of Wisdom

If you can write a tic-tac-toe game in Ruby that works, most people would agree that you know Ruby and that you have a clue about programming. It is not the easiest thing to do. If you grasp everything in this chapter, then you are ready to move beyond just an introduction to computer science.

Our tic-tac-toe game will not have a nice user interface. User interfaces are a more advanced topic that is beyond the scope of this book. We want you to focus on problem solving in this course and not on figuring out how to create a pretty user interface.

Our board will be drawn with simple X's and O's and will be invoked from the command line of your operating system.

We will first talk about how to approach the problem, and then how to implement the solution in an incremental fashion.

12.2 Programming Approach

First we need to break the problem into key steps. Many programmers are tempted to run to the computer and start writing code immediately and then debug their code. This is not recommended.

It is strongly suggested that you step away from the computer, grab paper and pencil, and write out the key algorithms that will be needed to solve the problem. As part of this effort, you should be able to describe the key objects and methods that will be involved.

The key steps of a tic-tac-toe game are rather straightforward. Until the board is full and there is no winner, do the following:

1. Draw the current board.
2. Ask the player for a move.
3. Make sure the move is valid (e.g., you can't move to a square that is already taken).
4. Store the current move.

You should write out the key objects and the key methods and then implement them gradually.

12.3 Tic-Tac-Toe

When two players initiate a game of tic-tac-toe, what is the first thing they do? They draw a board. Therefore, we will worry about the board first. A key object we will need is a Board object that stores the tic-tac-toe board. Think about the properties of such a

Gem of Wisdom

In Example 12-1, we use a shorthand way of declaring an array and its members. `Array.new(5) { 3 }` creates an array of five elements, with each value initialized to 3. Lines 8–10 declare an array (line 8), with each element being an array initialized to `EMPTY_POS` (line 9).

board. A board is typically a large square made up of 3 × 3 smaller squares. At the start of the game all the little squares will be empty, but later they will be filled in with X's and O's as the game progresses. Therefore, we will need a 3 × 3 array that is initially empty and can be filled in later while the game is being played. Using objects, we will be able to design the board construction.

Using our knowledge of arrays and objects, we are able to set up the board constructor as shown in Example 12-1.

Example 12-1. Initial board and constructor

```
 1 class Board
 2
 3   BOARD_MAX_INDEX = 2
 4   EMPTY_POS = ' '
 5
 6   def initialize(current_player)
 7     @current_player = current_player
 8     @board   = Array.new(BOARD_MAX_INDEX + 1) {
 9       Array.new(BOARD_MAX_INDEX + 1) { EMPTY_POS }
10     }
11   end
12 end
```

- Line 3 defines the largest index (remember, array indices start at 0).
- Line 4 defines what is considered an *empty position,* or a position not occupied by either an X or an O.
- Lines 6–11 define the constructor for our board.
- Line 7 assigns an instance variable that represents the current player.
- Lines 8–10 create the board instance variable, a 3 × 3 array.

The main program (*tictactoe.rb*) will use the board class. The start of the main program is given in Example 12-2.

Example 12-2. Beginning of tictactoe.rb

```
1 require_relative 'board.rb'
2
3 puts "Starting tic-tac-toe..."
4 players = ['X', 'O']
5 current_player = players[rand(2)]
6 b = Board.new(current_player)
7 b.display()
8 puts
```

- Lines 4 and 5 randomly pick an initial player (either X or O).

- Line 6 creates an instance of the Board class and assigns it to b.

- Lines 7 and 8 display the initial blank board and output a fresh blank line for readability.

The display method (which is part of *board.rb*) is given in Example 12-3.

Example 12-3. Display method for Board class

```
 1 def display
 2  puts "+- - - - - -+"
 3  for row in 0..BOARD_MAX_INDEX
 4   # print has to be used when we don't want to output a line break
 5   print "| "
 6   for col in 0..BOARD_MAX_INDEX
 7    s = @board[row][col]
 8    if s == EMPTY_POS
 9     print col + (row * 3) + 1
10    else
11     print s
12    end
13    print " | "
14   end
15   puts "\n+- - - - - -+"
16  end
17 end
```

- Line 2 prints a row of dashes (the top of the board).

- Line 3 starts an outer loop that runs through each row.

- Line 6 starts an inner loop that traverses each column.

- Line 7 assigns the current cell to the variable s.

- Lines 8–12 print the number of the cell if it's currently unoccupied or the current occupant if the cell is occupied.

Note the difference between print and puts: print simply writes the characters passed to it without writing an end of line upon completion. Thus, if one wishes to continue writing to a given line, print would be used. Remember, however, that if using print and a new line is desired, the newline character (\n) must be entered, as shown in line 15. This is in contrast to puts, which automatically inserts the newline character every time.

Returning to our main program, the key loop that runs the game will be implemented. The code is presented in Example 12-4. (The code begins at line 1; however, this is a continuation of *tictactoe.rb*.)

Example 12-4. Continuation of tictactoe.rb

```
 1 while not b.board_full() and not b.winner()
 2         b.ask_player_for_move(current_player)
 3         current_player = b.get_next_turn()
 4         b.display()
 5         puts
 6 end
 7
 8 if b.winner()
 9     puts "Player " +  b.get_next_turn() + " wins."
10 else
11     puts "Tie Game."
12 end
13 puts "Game Over"
```

- Line 1 starts a loop that continues as long as the board is not full and there is no winner.
- Line 2 prompts the current player for a move.
- Line 3 gets the next player.
- Lines 4 and 5 display the current board.
- Lines 8–13 print the winner's name if there was a winner, or "Tie Game" if the game ended in a tie.

The loop ends when there is a winner or there is a full board detected. At this point, you can see we need to discuss the board_full method, the winner method, and the get_next_turn method. The code presented in Example 12-5 is for the board_full method. This method determines if the board is full, meaning that no more pieces may be placed.

Example 12-5. board_full method

```
1 def board_full
2  for row in 0..BOARD_MAX_INDEX
3   for col in 0..BOARD_MAX_INDEX
4    if @board[row][col] == EMPTY_POS
5     return false
6    end
7   end
8  end
9  # Since we found no open positions, the board is full
10 return true
11 end
```

- Line 4 checks each cell to see if it is unoccupied. If at least one cell is unoccupied, the board is not full and the game must continue.

- Line 10 returns true in the event that none of the cells are open for possible capture.

The winner method is more complex. Essentially, we must check every row, every column, and every diagonal for a winner. The method is presented in Example 12-6.

Example 12-6. Winner method

```
1  def winner
2   winner = winner_rows()
3   if winner
4    return winner
5   end
6   winner = winner_cols()
7   if winner
8    return winner
9   end
10  winner = winner_diagonals()
11  if winner
12   return winner
13  end
14  # No winners
15  return
16 end
```

The winner method uses the helper methods winner_rows, winner_cols, and winner_diagonals, which return the player's symbol if the player won by connecting the rows, columns, or diagonals with her or his pieces, respectively. If winner is set, then we know that the current value of winner is the player who won the game. Otherwise, we return nothing, signifying there is no winner yet.

The methods winner_rows, winner_cols, and winner_diagonals are good examples of class methods, as explained in Chapter 9. They are all fairly straightforward, as they all look for three of the same values with regard to their given task. The method winner_rows is shown in Example 12-7.

Gem of Wisdom

Aside from being able to return values, the return keyword immediately stops execution of the current method and returns to the one from which it was called. This is used heavily in the winner method. If the winner is found in the rows, the columns and diagonals are not searched. Likewise, if the winner is found in the columns, the diagonals are not searched.

Example 12-7. winner_rows method

```
 1 def winner_rows
 2  for row_index in 0..BOARD_MAX_INDEX
 3   first_symbol = @board[row_index][0]
 4   for col_index in 1..BOARD_MAX_INDEX
 5    if first_symbol != @board[row_index][col_index]
 6      break
 7    elsif col_index == BOARD_MAX_INDEX and first_symbol != EMPTY_POS
 8      return first_symbol
 9    end
10   end
11  end
12  return
13 end
```

- Line 2 begins an outer loop to look for a winner across a row. For each row, all the columns are checked. The variable first_symbol contains the symbol that must match.

- Line 3 initializes first_symbol for row 0.

- Lines 4–10 provide an inner loop that looks at all elements in the given column. If a cell does not match the first_symbol value, then it is not a winning combination.

  For example, if the first_symbol value was initially an O and now we encounter an X in the same column, then this is not a winning combination. If we reach the end of the columns, we have a winner, and we return the winner as its name is in the first_symbol column.

- Line 7 contains a final check to make sure we have not found three empty positions in a column. If we do not return a winner, then we simply return on line 12 (this is essentially returning a nil or false value) to the caller of this method.

The next method, presented in Example 12-8, is very similar in that it looks for a winning column. This time, a given column is checked, and we travel down the column checking to see if we have all matching symbols.

Example 12-8. winner_cols method

```
 1 def winner_cols
 2  for col_index in 0..BOARD_MAX_INDEX
 3   first_symbol = @board[0][col_index]
 4   for row_index in 1..BOARD_MAX_INDEX
 5    if first_symbol != @board[row_index][col_index]
 6     break
 7    elsif row_index == BOARD_MAX_INDEX and first_symbol != EMPTY_POS
 8     return first_symbol
 9    end
10   end
11  end
12  return
13 end
```

Finally, we look for a win across a diagonal. This is inherently more difficult because it requires a backward traversal of the columns. This is done with the `winner_diagonals` method shown in Example 12-9.

Example 12-9. winner_diagonals method

```
 1 def winner_diagonals
 2  first_symbol = @board[0][0]
 3  for index in 1..BOARD_MAX_INDEX
 4   if first_symbol != @board[index][index]
 5    break
 6   elsif index == BOARD_MAX_INDEX and first_symbol != EMPTY_POS
 7    return first_symbol
 8   end
 9  end
10  first_symbol = @board[0][BOARD_MAX_INDEX]
11  row_index = 0
12  col_index = BOARD_MAX_INDEX
13  while row_index < BOARD_MAX_INDEX
14   row_index = row_index + 1
15   col_index = col_index - 1
16   if first_symbol != @board[row_index][col_index]
17    break
18   elsif row_index == BOARD_MAX_INDEX and first_symbol != EMPTY_POS
19    return first_symbol
20   end
21  end
22  return
23 end
```

- Line 2 initializes our search with the upper-lefthand corner of the board.

- Lines 3–9 traverse the diagonal from the top left to the bottom right, continuing as long as there is a match.

- Line 10 sets the initial value to the top right.

- Lines 11–20 check the diagonal from the top right to the bottom left. If no matches are found, we return nothing (line 22).

The only methods we have not yet described are the `ask_player_for_move` method and the `validate_position` method, which simply prompt the user for a move and ensures that the move is allowed. The `ask_player_for_move` method is presented in Example 12-10.

Example 12-10. ask_player_for_move method

```
 1 def ask_player_for_move(current_player)
 2   played = false
 3   while not played
 4     puts "Player " + current_player + ": Where would you like to play?"
 5     move = gets.to_i - 1
 6     col = move % @board.size
 7     row = (move - col) / @board.size
 8     if validate_position(row, col)
 9       @board[row][col] = current_player
10       played = true
11     end
12   end
13 end
```

- Line 3 starts a loop that keeps processing until a valid move is obtained. The flag `played` is initially set to `false`.

- Line 4 asks the user for her or his move.

- Line 5 obtains the user's response with a call to `gets`, which obtains a string and then converts it to an integer.

- Line 6 converts the number 1–9 into column number 0–2, and line 7 converts it into a row number. These conversions stem from the equation that took each cell of the array and assigned a cell number. Convince yourself that lines 6 and 7 are correct.

- Line 8 calls another internal method, `validate_position`, which is a method that makes sure the user chooses a spot on the board and a spot that is not already taken. If a valid position is obtained, then line 10 sets the `played` flag to be `true`, and the loop will end when line 3 is encountered. For an invalid move, the `played` flag is not set to `true`, so the loop will continue again.

The `validate_position` method is given in Example 12-11.

Example 12-11. validate_position method

```
 1 def validate_position(row, col)
 2  if row <= @board.size and col <= @board.size
 3   if @board[row][col] == EMPTY_POS
 4     return true
 5   else
 6     puts "That position is occupied."
 7   end
 8  else
 9    puts "Invalid position."
10  end
11  return false
12 end
```

- Line 2 makes sure the row and column are within the range of the board. We know it's a three row by three column game, but by using the `size` variable we could easily expand this to larger board sizes for other games, like Connect Four. In this case the size is three elements, 0, 1, and 2. The size was established earlier, but this will allow us to easily change the size of the board.

- Line 3 checks to make sure the user has selected a position that was previously empty. If so, `true` is returned, and we are done.

- Lines 5–7 handle the case for when a user selects an occupied position.

- Lines 8–10 handle the case for when a user selects a position off the board.

- Line 11 returns `false`, which indicates that an invalid move occurred. Note that line 11 is reached only when an invalid move is attempted.

Finally, we need to discuss the `get_next_turn` method, and we are done. It is very simple and is shown in Example 12-12.

Example 12-12. get_next_turn_method

```
 1 def get_next_turn
 2  if @current_player == 'X'
 3   @current_player = 'O'
 4  else
 5   @current_player = 'X'
 6  end
 7  return @current_player
 8 end
```

- Line 2 checks to see if we were using an X, and if so, we change to the O in line 3; otherwise, it was an O, so in line 5 we turn it into an X.

At this point, we have created a working game of tic-tac-toe that you can play against yourself or a friend. The code written for this game encompasses almost all the topics covered in this book. If you understood it all, give yourself a pat on the back. If you are frustrated with this chapter and do not understand all the ideas presented, it is a good idea to go back to previous chapters and play around with the Ruby concepts presented in those chapters.

Don't get too comfortable if you've done well thus far. The next section will add artificial intelligence to our tic-tac-toe game, enabling you to play against the computer.

12.4 Tic-Tac-Toe Revised

Although a player-versus-player version of tic-tac-toe is nice, chances are you will not have a friend who wants to spend time playing computerized tic-tac-toe with you for long. Perhaps it will be more satisfying if you create a version of tic-tac-toe that will play against you. This is what we will do in this section.

First, let's understand the change we are trying to make. Instead of always having the player input the position on the board to fill, we want the computer to take one of the turns. Therefore, we will make a clearer distinction between the human's move and the computer's move. The code in Example 12-13 illustrates this change.

Example 12-13. Revised ask_player_for_move method

```
1 def ask_player_for_move(current_player)
2   if current_player == COMPUTER_PLAYER
3     computer_move(current_player)
4   else
5     human_move(current_player)
6   end
7 end
```

The purpose of the ask_player_for_move method is to switch between player input and computer AI (artificial intelligence) based on the current player. If the current player is the computer (line 2), let the computer take its move (line 3); otherwise (line 4), let the user take her or his move (line 5). Make sure to define the constant COMPUTER_PLAYER. It may be set equal to X or O. This would also be a good time to define the constant HUMAN_PLAYER. This should be set equal to O if COMPUTER_PLAYER is equal to X, or X if COMPUTER_PLAYER is equal to O.

If you have been reading carefully, you will have noticed that ask_player_for_move was already defined pages ago, and now we have changed its definition here. Previously, the method prompted either player one or player two for which turn she or he wanted to make, and then took the turn if it was valid. That code was relocated to the method human_move. The code for human_move is identical to our old ask_player_for_move method.

At this point, we have a mechanism for changing between the human's and the computer's turn, and we have slightly changed the definition of the human's turn. From here it should be clear that the next logical step is to define the computer_move method, and it is defined in Example 12-14.

Example 12-14. computer_move method

```
1 def computer_move(current_player)
2   row = -1
3   col = -1
4   found = "F"
5
6   check_rows(COMPUTER_PLAYER, found)
7   check_cols(COMPUTER_PLAYER, found)
8   check_diagonals(COMPUTER_PLAYER, found)
9
10  check_rows(HUMAN_PLAYER, found)
11  check_cols(HUMAN_PLAYER, found)
12  check_diagonals(HUMAN_PLAYER, found)
13
14  if found == "F"
15    if @board[1][1] == EMPTY_POS
16      row = 1
17      col = 1
18      @board[row][col] = current_player
19    elsif available_corner()
20      pick_corner(current_player)
21    else
22      until validate_position(row, col)
23        row = rand(@board.size)
24        col = rand(@board.size)
25      end
26      @board[row][col] = current_player
27    end
28  end
29 end
```

If this method looks complicated, don't worry. First, let's walk through the code at an algorithmic level. The computer_move method does the following in order, picking the first rule it can successfully complete:

1. Check the rows, columns, and diagonals to see if either the computer can win or the human can win. If such a spot exists, take it to either win the game or prevent the human from winning. Note that we intentionally do not include the code for those methods, as their implementation is straightforward and their details are unnecessary for the purposes of our discussion.

2. If the middle cell is unoccupied, take the middle cell.

3. If there is an available corner, take any of the available corner spots.

4. If none of the prior conditions are true, pick a random cell.

For simplicity, we did not include all the necessary code to guarantee at least a draw for the AI. However, in tic-tac-toe, correct play guarantees at least a draw. To guarantee *at least* a draw, the computer's corner selection option should be modified as follows:

If a corner spot is available, then select a corner spot, with the following corner selection preference. If the computer went first, randomly choose among the available corners that are not adjacent to the human's noncenter spot(s). If the human went first, then check for one exception condition; otherwise, randomly choose among the available corners that are adjacent to the human's noncenter spot(s). The exception condition is one in which only three squares are occupied, the computer has the center square, and the human has both corners on the same diagonal; in such a case, override the corner selection option and randomly choose a noncorner spot. If none of the aforementioned conditions are met, then choose any available corner.

This description defines a high-level algorithm for the game of tic-tac-toe. You now have all the needed skills to design, develop, and debug all the implementation specifics. Please do so and enjoy playing your computerized opponent.

12.5 Summary

Now that we have walked through a more detailed example, you should be able to implement some fun games in Ruby. Games like blackjack and poker are now all within your grasp.

We have combined the concepts covered in the previous chapters in this example. With the file processing we discussed in Chapter 11, you can even make it so that you can save the state of these games or the current high score to a file. These concepts are common among most programming languages. So, as a programmer, it is much more effective to learn these concepts and how they can be used to solve certain problems than to direct your focus onto learning syntax, which is just the tool that allows us to implement our ideas.

The best way to become more comfortable with these types of problems is to practice doing them. Take your time with the following problems, draw out what the problem requires, and design a solution. Eventually, this process becomes much easier, and you will be able to implement the solution in any language.

12.6 Exercises

1. Give a detailed explanation of the relationship between the board and the tic-tac-toe objects.

2. Design and implement a game of "pick a number." This is a simple guessing game where you think of a number between 1 and *n* in your head (don't let the computer know this number). Tell the computer what *n* is, and then let the computer guess the number. If the guess is too low, you should let the computer know that the guess was too low; likewise, if the guess was too high you should also let the computer know. The computer can take multiple turns (hint: it should take log *n* turns), but simply guessing every number between 1 and *n* is far from an acceptable answer. Implement this program two different ways: procedurally and object-oriented.

3. Design and implement a simplified version of the card game blackjack. The rules are as follows:

   a. A standard 52-card deck is used and shuffled well.

   b. The cards have the following values: 2 to 10 are the value of the card, jack to king have a value of 10, and ace has a value of 1 or 11.

   c. Only you are playing, trying to get the cards to add up to 21 without going over 21. If you go over 21, you lose.

   d. Initially you are dealt two cards. If you are dissatisfied with these cards, you can ask for more. It is not a trade; additional cards are added. If you feel like you have enough cards and do not want to bust, you can "stay" and end this round of blackjack.

   After the game has ended, the user should be able to play again, if she or he chooses to do so. If so, the game will restart like a brand-new game. Implement this in an OO fashion. If you split the work among your objects properly, you will be able to reuse a significant chunk of code on the next problem.

4. Add scoreboard functionality to Exercise 3. To do this, you need to make a few game modifications. First, you need to ask for the user's name at the beginning of every game. Next, you need the ability to view the scoreboard during a game; this should be done directly after prompting for a name. If a user's name already exists on the scoreboard, you will modify that user's score. Otherwise, the new user will be added to the scoreboard in the proper position. The scoreboard needs to remember scores even after the program is exited (hint: write scores out to a file). If a score surpasses another score, the ordering of scores on the scoreboard needs to change. The highest score should be listed first, the lowest score last. The scoring criteria are defined in Table 12-1.

Table 12-1. Blackjack scoring criteria

Total card value	Points given
Bust	−15
21	40
20	30
19	20
18	10
17	5
16	1
< 16	0

5. Being able to read and modify other people's code is essential to being a successful computer scientist. Modify *tictactoe.rb* and *board.rb* to play tic-tac-toe on boards of size 3 × 3, 6 × 6, and 9 × 9 based on the user's choice. Adjust everything so that the game works as well on 6 × 6 and 9 × 9 boards as it does on 3 × 3 boards.

6. The current AI for the tic-tac-toe game is not perfect. Implement the behavior discussed in this chapter's summary to guarantee at least a draw, and ensure its correctness.

Recommended Additional Reading

A.1 OS Reading Material

- *Modern Operating Systems* by Andrew S. Tanenbaum (Prentice Hall). *http://bit.ly/XHecjo*
- *Computer Systems: A Programmer's Perspective* by Randal E. Bryant and David R. O'Hallaron (Addison-Wesley). *http://csapp.cs.cmu.edu/*
- *Lions' Commentary on UNIX, 6th Edition*, with Source Code by John Lions. *http://bit.ly/YQ1VrJ*

A.2 Ruby Documentation

- Ruby API documentation (*http://ruby-doc.org/core/*)
- *Programming Ruby 1.9, The Pragmatic Programmers' Guide, 3rd Edition* by Dave Thomas, with Chad Fowler and Andy Hunt (Pragmatic Bookshelf). *http://bit.ly/10QnLt0*
- *Metaprogramming Ruby* by Paolo Perrotta (Pragmatic Bookshelf). *http://bit.ly/10QnNkt*
- *The Ruby Programming Language* by David Flanagan and Yukihiro Matsumoto (O'Reilly). *http://oreil.ly/1534yK7*

A.3 Algorithm and Complexity Reading Material

- *Introduction to Algorithms, 3rd Edition* by Thomas Cormen, Charles Leiserson, Ronald Rivest, and Clifford Stein (MIT Press). *http://bit.ly/XHeN4A*

- *Algorithms in a Nutshell* by George Heineman, Gary Pollice, and Stanley Selkow (O'Reilly). *http://oreil.ly/16ROhGd*

- *Introduction to the Design and Analysis Algorithms, 3rd Edition* by Anany Levitin (Addison-Wesley Longman, Inc.). *http://bit.ly/10ZXCbw*

Installing Ruby

This book uses the Ruby programming language to demonstrate code. It is expected that the student learn how to develop programs in Ruby. To accomplish such, the Ruby language must be installed.

To install Ruby on your computer, follow the instructions that correspond to your operating system (Windows, Mac, or Linux).

B.1 Windows

1. Open a web browser and go to the Ruby Installer (*http://rubyinstaller.org/*).
2. Click the Download button on the main page.
3. Click the top file under RubyInstallers and save the file to the desktop.
4. Double-click the file on the desktop and follow the instructions to install Ruby. `irb` will automatically be installed with the package, as will the rdocs.

B.2 Linux

Debian/Ubuntu: `$ sudo apt-get install ruby1.9.1-full`

Gentoo: `$ emerge ruby irb rdoc`

Slackware: Download the source code (*http://www.ruby-lang.org*) and follow the instructions in the *tar.gz* file.

B.3 Mac OS X

Ruby is installed by default in Mac OS X. However, we recommend that you update to a later version of Ruby 1.9 by using the One-Click install (*http://rubyosx.rubyforge.org/*).

Writing Code for Ruby

This appendix describes tools that will make writing Ruby code easier. Utilities that provide syntax highlighting and code indentation make it easier for you to focus on the code you are writing.

C.1 Windows

Most Windows users will prefer to use Edit Plus 2, a text editor that uses syntax highlighting. This utility can be found at *http://www.editplus.com*. On the main page, click on Download Latest Version and follow the installation instructions. There are also syntax highlighting files on the website, which you will need to download for syntax highlighting in Ruby. These can be found under the Features section. Follow download and install instructions provided by the website.

C.2 Linux

Linux users usually have two choices when it comes to full-featured text editors: emacs and vim (*http://www.vim.org/*). We will discuss vim here, but additional information on emacs can be found on Google by searching for emacs. Vim is a fully customizable text editor that offers out-of-the-box syntax highlighting for nearly every language. To learn how to use vim, type the following in the command line:

```
$ vimtutor
```

This text editor will teach you how to use all the commands in vim. You may want to customize vim before jumping in, so in your *home* directory, create a new file:

```
$ vim ~/.vimrc
```

and add the lines:

```
set number
syntax on
set nowrap
set tabstop=4
```

Then type :wq and press Enter to save and quit.

For a more comprehensive tutorial, read *Learning the vi and Vim Editors* by Arnold Robbins, Elbert Hannah, and Linda Lamb (O'Reilly).

C.3 Mac OS X

TextMate (*http://macromates.com/*) is a wonderful (though not free) programming solution. It offers syntax highlighting, macros, and a very intuitive and easy interface. Mac users who do not wish to pay for a text editing suite may also use vim in Terminal (in Applications→Utilities). See the Linux section on getting started with that.

C.4 General Information

- Ruby files have the extension *.rb*.
- To run a Ruby program, either double-click the file or use the command line (assuming the Ruby interpreter executable is in your PATH):

```
$ ruby program.rb
```

Using irb

Oftentimes while programming, you will wonder about the syntax of a command or how something works in Ruby. Creating a new file and running it is the wrong option in many cases because it wastes a lot of time.

irb is Ruby's interactive interpreter (short for Interactive Ruby). This is a great tool that you will want to learn to use, as it will greatly speed up time spent debugging code. We also use it throughout the book to give examples.

To run irb, first open a terminal.

In Windows, you can do this by opening the Start menu and clicking on Run. A small window will appear with a text box. Type cmd and hit Return. A black-and-white window that has a blinking cursor will open. Welcome to the terminal.

On a Mac, the Terminal is located in Applications→Utilities.

Type irb in the terminal to launch irb. When it launches, you will be greeted with a prompt to enter your first line of code:

```
irb(main):001:0>
```

To exit, either type exit or hit Ctrl-D. This is a terminating condition that allows you to exit most programs.

About the Authors

Ophir Frieder holds the Robert L. McDevitt, K.S.G., K.C.H.S., and Catherine H. McDevitt L.C.H.S. Chair in Computer Science and Information Processing and is Chair of the Department of Computer Science at Georgetown University. He is also Professor of Biostatistics, Bioinformatics, and Biomathematics in the Georgetown University Medical Center. He is a Fellow of the AAAS, ACM, and IEEE.

Gideon Frieder is the former Dean of Engineering and currently A. James Clark Professor Emeritus of Engineering and Applied Science in the School of Engineering of George Washington University. Author of various academic publications in areas of physics, logic, medical applications, and computer design, his background includes industrial and academic development of sophisticated projects such as complex systems (in the Israeli DoD), an innovative universal emulator/computer used, among other applications, in the certification of the Trident Submarine firing systems (in the United States, via industrial corporations), and the design of a solar car that won first place in the 1995 World Solar Challenge in Japan. In all cases, the development was from the "gleam in the eye" phase through basic research, followed by development, design, certification, and prototype.

David Grossman is the Associate Director of the Information Retrieval Lab at Georgetown University and the Chair of the Steering Committee for the ACM Conference on Information and Knowledge Management. Previously, he was an Associate Professor of Computer Science and the Director of the Information Retrieval Laboratory at the Illinois Institute of Technology. He was a Principal Investigator on several NSF grants that solely focused on improving the computer science undergraduate curriculum. He also chaired, for more than six years, the IIT Computer Science Undergraduate Studies Committee and led the department through two successful ABET reviews. He has taught computer science courses at all levels (freshman through Ph.D. seminars) at IIT, the University of Maryland, George Washington University, and George Mason University.

Colophon

The animal on the cover of *Computer Science Programming Basics in Ruby* is a common Creeper.

The cover image is from Cassell's *Natural History*. The cover font is Adobe ITC Garamond. The text font is Adobe Minion Pro; the heading font is Adobe Myriad Condensed; and the code font is Dalton Maag's Ubuntu Mono.

Get even more for your money.

Join the O'Reilly Community, and register the O'Reilly books you own. It's free, and you'll get:

- $4.99 ebook upgrade offer
- 40% upgrade offer on O'Reilly print books
- Membership discounts on books and events
- Free lifetime updates to ebooks and videos
- Multiple ebook formats, DRM FREE
- Participation in the O'Reilly community
- Newsletters
- Account management
- 100% Satisfaction Guarantee

Signing up is easy:

1. **Go to: oreilly.com/go/register**
2. **Create an O'Reilly login.**
3. **Provide your address.**
4. **Register your books.**

Note: English-language books only

To order books online:
oreilly.com/store

For questions about products or an order:
orders@oreilly.com

To sign up to get topic-specific email announcements and/or news about upcoming books, conferences, special offers, and new technologies:
elists@oreilly.com

For technical questions about book content:
booktech@oreilly.com

To submit new book proposals to our editors:
proposals@oreilly.com

O'Reilly books are available in multiple DRM-free ebook formats. For more information:
oreilly.com/ebooks

O'REILLY®

Spreading the knowledge of innovators   oreilly.com

©2010 O'Reilly Media, Inc. O'Reilly logo is a registered trademark of O'Reilly Media, Inc. 00000

CPSIA information can be obtained
at www.ICGtesting.com
Printed in the USA
BVOW04s0843250717

490110BV00011B/28/P